A Hero's Walk
The World War II Journey of Lt. B.B. Darnell

Mike Darnell

The author, Mike Darnell, is a college class mate and friend of Susan Sanders Baxter. War Eagle!

:

"The war in Italy was tough. The land and the weather were both against us. It rained and it rained. Vehicles bogged down and bridges washed out. The country was shockingly beautiful, and just as shockingly hard to capture from the enemy."

- Ernie Pyle in "Brave Men", 1944

CONTENTS

CONTENTS

The Italian Campaign

(*Excerpted from History.com*)

In Casablanca, Morocco, in January 1943, Allied leaders decided to use their massive military resources in the Mediterranean to launch an invasion of Italy, which British Prime Minister Winston Churchill called the "soft underbelly of Europe." The objectives were to remove Italy from World War II, secure the Mediterranean Sea and force Germany to divert some divisions from the Russian front and other German divisions from northern France, where the Allies were planning their cross-Channel landing at Normandy, France.

On July 10, 1943, Operation Husky, the code name for the invasion of Sicily, began with airborne and amphibious landings on the island's southern shores. Jarred by the Allied invasion, the Italian fascist regime fell rapidly into disrepute, as the Allies had hoped. On July 24, 1943, Prime Minister Benito Mussolini was deposed and arrested. A new provisional government was set up under Marshal Pietro Badoglio, who had opposed Italy's alliance with Nazi Germany and who immediately began secret discussions with the Allies about an armistice.

Meanwhile, the German command deployed 16 new divisions on the Italian mainland. German leader Adolf Hitler did not want to let the Allies establish air bases in Italy that could threaten Germany's southern cities as well as its primary oil supplies in Romania. He instructed his army group commander in southern Italy, Field Marshal Albert Kesselring, to make the Allies pay dearly for every inch of their advance.

On September 9, 1943, when American troops landed on the Italian coast at Salerno, the German army, which was rapidly taking over the defense of Italy, nearly drove them back into the Tyrrhenian Sea. Germans entrenched in the high Apennine Mountains at Cassino brought the mobile Allied army to a grinding halt for four months. An intended quick push inland at Anzio became bogged down in driving rains, German air raids and command hesitation, prompting Churchill to complain, "I had hoped we were hurling a wildcat onto the shore, but all we got was a stranded whale." Where the mountains receded, there were still muddy rolling hills, flooded rivers and washed-out roads to hamper the Allied advance and assist the German defenders. Under the resourceful Commander Kesselring, German forces set up several defensive lines across the narrow Italian peninsula. The southernmost of these, the Gustav Line, ran just behind Monte Cassino. Despite Allied air superiority across Italy, it took Allied soldiers four grueling battles over several months to break through heavily fortified Gustav Line.

As General Clark's Fifth U.S. Army moved into Rome on June 4, 1944, the D-Day landings in Normandy, scheduled for June 6, took priority over the Italian Campaign. Six Allied divisions were removed from Italy to support landings in southern France. Further Allied advances in Italy were slow and hampered by heavy autumn rains. The Allied High Command ordered that priority be given to pinning down as many German divisions as possible for the duration of the war, rather than pressing the Italian offensive further. Allied soldiers had pushed across the Po Valley in northern Italy when German forces in Italy finally surrendered on May 2, 1945, two days after the collapse of Berlin.

The Allied campaign in Italy, launched with some optimism after the Allied victory in North Africa in 1943, turned into a brutal, protracted, and costly slog. American casualties at Anzio alone were 59,000. The difficult combat pushed many soldiers to their breaking point. The battle for Italy became an extended bloodletting between tenacious Allied troops and steadfast German forces. It ended only when the war in Europe ended. By then, more than 300,000 U.S. and British troops who fought in Italy had been killed or were wounded or missing. German casualties totaled around 434,000.

Medals Awarded to Lt. B. B. Darnell in WWII

Silver Star   The United States third highest military decoration for valor. It is awarded for gallantry in action against an enemy of the United States. Lt. Darnell earned the Silver Star for his actions during combat in May, 1944, near Castellonorato, Italy.

Bronze Oak Leaf Cluster to Silver Star   Awarded in lieu of a second Silver Star for gallantry in action against an enemy of the United States. Lt. Darnell was awarded this for his actions in combat in the northern Apennine Mountains in September/October, 1944.

Bronze Star   Awarded with a "V" for valor. The United States Army's fourth highest military award for heroism in a combat zone. Lt. Darnell was awarded the Bronze Star for his actions under fire, assisting a fellow soldier whose arm had been severed by shrapnel in September, 1944.

Purple Heart   Awarded for wounds suffered in combat against an enemy of the United States. Lt. Darnell was wounded in action on October 12, 1944, in northern Italy,

American Campaign Medal   A service medal recognizing U.S. military members who performed active duty in the American Theater of Operations during World War II.

European-Africa-Middle Eastern Campaign Medal   A service medal recognizing members of the U.S. military who performed duty in the European Theater during World War II.

World War II Victory Medal   A service medal recognizing U.S. military members who served during World War II.

Army of Occupation Medal (Germany)   A service medal recognizing U.S. military members who performed 30 or more consecutive days of duty in Germany, Austria, or Italy after World War II.

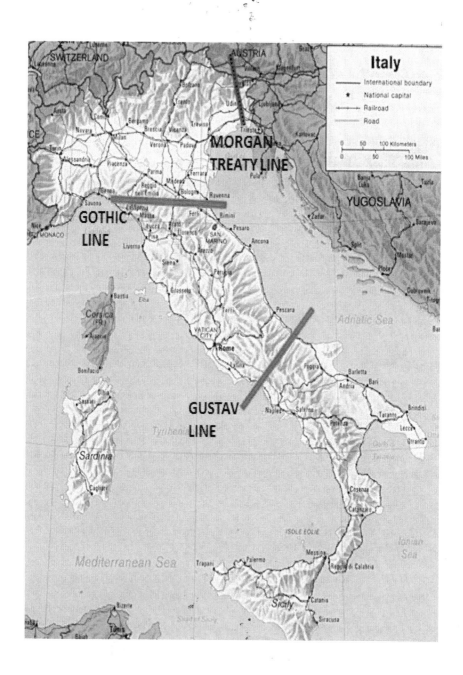

PREFACE

Young boys often consider their fathers heroes, and I was no different.   But as I became older, I realized that B.B. Darnell really was a hero.

One definition of a hero is "a *person who is admired for courage, outstanding achievements, or noble qualities*".

I admired my father for his noble qualities – chief among them were his faith, honesty, and integrity.   During my search for information about his service overseas during World War II, I discovered details of his courage that no one in our family was aware.

Although he was highly decorated for his actions in World War II, he never really talked much about that. Over the course of my lifetime with him, there was an occasional anecdote about his time overseas, and in his last years he expressed regrets about the horrors he had seen, but there was never much detail.   And as young men often do, I was too busy living my life to ask the right questions at the right times to learn what he really experienced.

So in order to recreate some of my father's time overseas, I depended on help from a multitude of sources and months and months of research.   Unfortunately, I have only been able to find one letter that he wrote during his time overseas and that was to his Aunt Flossie. There is a postcard to my mother, prior to their marriage, while he was preparing to go overseas, and then two letters and a postcard to her while at Ft. Bliss during the Korean Conflict.   These helped provide insight, but that is the extent of his correspondence that I have located.

His "constructed" overseas journal is fictitious, but factual, based on my knowledge of the man and my research. I attempted to write it as he would have written. The facts have been gleaned from obtaining his military records from the Army, his occasional remarks over the years, unit histories, operational reports, various first-hand accounts from soldiers, and other historical documents.

In addition, I was able to travel to Italy in 2014 and trace most of the route Daddy traveled through the country. I found several of the places he would have been and where specific actions occurred. It was an amazing experience to realize that, I was walking where he fought 70 years earlier. I will never forget my conversations with the Italians who expressed to me how grateful they were to the American soldiers who liberated their country

I was fortunate about six weeks before his death in 2011, to have had a conversation with my father and mother about how they met, dating, and the events that occurred after he arrived back home in Alabama. It was a rare moment of clarity near the end of his life. That conversation and the look in their eyes as they talked (with my oldest son & his wife present) will always be one of my greatest treasures. I knew I had to share that story here as well.

I am grateful for all the sacrifices my parents made during their lifetimes so that I and my children might have a better life. Daddy's time in the Army during World War II is just one of those sacrifices. It is a story worth telling. It is a story I had to tell.

Second Lieutenant B.B. Darnell in the fall of 1943 prior to shipping overseas

I Can Remember

I can remember quiet . . .
So still that I could hear the breeze blowing through the cotton
stalks in the field.
.

I can remember warm . . .
Gliding on the front porch swing . . .
The Sunday sun just beginning to warm the cool morning air.

I can remember happiness . . .
Your face…
Your head back...
Smiling about some secret we had just shared.

But I am here . . .
With the thunder of battle that never stops . . .
I am cold . . .
I am wet . . .
I am suffocated by the smell of death . . .
The smell of a young man's fear.

But I can remember . . . .
I CAN remember.

Susan Sanders Baxter, 2015
Inspired by Lt. B.B. Darnell's World War II Journey

A Hero's Walk

CHAPTER ONE
HOME AT LAST

November 9, 1945

The little town of Notasulga, Alabama, never looked as good as it did on that cool fall morning in 1945 when Lt. B.B. Darnell stepped off the Atlanta & West Point Railroad train and onto the wooden station platform in his home town. After 22 months overseas, he was finally back home, alive and well.

Even though he had been on the train for hours, he still looked sharp in his Army uniform. B.B. was just one of many soldiers on that train, but the only one who got off at the Notasulga station.

As he looked down the platform, he saw his father, Marshall, waiting for him. They both smiled broadly as they walked toward each other, shook hands, and then hugged. Marshall wasn't known for being overly demonstrative with his affections, but B.B. could see a mist in his eyes when he said "Welcome home, son. I missed you." Overcome by his own emotions for a moment, B.B. just hugged his father, holding tight to his father's large frame. The two men embraced for a long moment with no need to say anything.

"Let's go now," Marshall said as he broke the embrace. "The women have been cooking since early this morning, so I hope you're ready for a big dinner!" "Yes sir," B.B. replied, "I have been looking forward to that ever since I left!"

B.B. threw his duffle bag into the back of his father's pickup truck and a few minutes later, his boyhood home was in sight.

As they pulled into the dirt driveway at the house, B.B. smiled as he saw the big white oak tree that had been there as long as he could remember. And then the smaller magnolia tree right behind it that his mother had planted when he was little. "Looks like the magnolia tree has grown some while I was gone", B.B. said. Marshall smiled, "Yeah, trees tend to grow better when teenagers aren't running over them in my truck." His daddy still had that dry sense of humor.

As they stepped into the house, B.B. was just about overcome with the familiar warmth of home, and the smells of his favorite foods coming from the kitchen. It was the first time he had been back since his mother passed away and his father had remarried. Being there at that moment made him miss her more than ever. If only he could hug her at this moment. He missed her so much.

A second later, with a rustle of noise and joy, the apron-clad women came from the kitchen led by his father's sister, Flossie. They welcomed him home with hugs, tears, and kisses. He met Marshall's new wife Effie for the first time while Aunt Flossie and Carl's wife Francis were fussing over him. And then there was Carl's four-year old daughter Carol. It wasn't long before the little red-headed girl warmed up to her Uncle B.B. and had him wrapped around her finger. It was good to be home. The noon meal time was filled with catching up and lots of laughter as B.B. enjoyed the home-cooked meal and being with his family. The war seemed a long way away, finally.

After the meal, B.B. and his father took a long walk over the farm and talked. It was good to be walking on the land where he grew up. There had been lots of times during the last couple of years, B.B. wasn't sure he would ever see it again, so this walk with his father was special. They talked about farming, about the community, what had been going on since B.B. left, and a little about his time overseas. Marshall filled B.B. in on what he knew about Carl's war injury. B.B. learned his brother was on a hospital ship off the coast of China, lucky to be alive.

As they headed back to the house, B.B. asked, "Daddy, can I borrow your truck? I want to go see some folks." Marshall looked at him and smiled, "By folks, do you mean Mildred?" B.B.'s face reddened slightly. "Of course you can use the truck. You know she was always your momma's favorite."

So with that B.B. headed east toward Opelika, hoping to catch Mildred as she got off work at the telephone company. He hadn't called Mildred to tell her he would be home today. He wanted to surprise her.

As he drove through Loachapoka, he saw his cousin, A.B. Williams, working out in front of their family's store, so he pulled in to say hello.

A.B. knew his cousin well enough to guess where he was headed. "Mildred is over at her parents' house this weekend," A.B. informed him. "George Dawson came by this morning and told me he was taking her to the picture show tonight."

"She doesn't know I'm home yet," B.B. responded.

"Well, you need to go see her – right now," his cousin prodded.

B.B.'s thoughts were swirling with that news. This wasn't exactly the homecoming he had planned with Mildred. "I should have called her yesterday!" he thought.

But A.B. was right, he did need to go see her and see her right now. While he and Mildred hadn't made any long term commitments before he left for the war, B.B. had made some decisions when he was overseas. And the biggest one was about Mildred. He knew he loved her and it was time to do something about it.

So the young soldier hurriedly said goodbye and hopped in the old truck. He left his cousin grinning in a cloud of dust as he sped away.

"I didn't go halfway around the world, fight a war and come home to lose the only girl I ever loved," thought B.B. as he set his jaw and turned across the railroad tracks onto Beehive Road.

Mildred Moore circa 1938

CHAPTER TWO
THE JOURNAL BEGINS

24 Dec 1943

Early this morning, we loaded onto the USS General Alexander E. Anderson at the naval yard in Newport News, VA. My first time ever on a ship this big. It's Christmas Eve.

We were herded like cattle, down Pier 6, up the steep gangway, with our duffel bags, packs, weapons, & steel helmets into a big hole in the side of a big ship. There were ladies there from the Red Cross giving all the soldiers coffee and doughnuts. We loaded in the dark for security, so we never really got to even see the ship before we boarded. I wish I could say it was one of those fancy pleasure cruises I've read about. I expect it to be anything but that, wherever we are going. There are about 6000 of us from the 85th Division on here. After everybody got squared away, we finally steamed out about mid-day.

We came down from Ft. Dix, NJ, a couple of weeks ago and have been stationed at Ft. Patrick Henry. It was obvious to everybody that we were getting ready to ship overseas...but nobody knew exactly when or where. It was a sobering moment when we were ordered to make our wills, assign a personal power of attorney and sign an embarkation form. And the shots...they must have inoculated us for every disease known to man!

Some say we are headed through the Panama Canal to the Pacific, while others say England, and some say North Africa. I don't think it is the Pacific, because we were in southern

California training two months ago. Seems like they would have just shipped us out then if we were headed to the Pacific Theater. But none of us really know. Spirits are good and everybody is excited, but none of us know what to expect. While ready for whatever we have to do, deep down, I think everyone is a little uneasy about what is ahead. It was a strange feeling as we pulled away from American shores.

The entire 85th Division will be leaving during the next couple of days, but today it's just the 339th Infantry and the 328th Field Artillery Battalion. Our 105s, trucks, and heavy equipment are supposed to be wherever it is we are headed.

Seas were rough as we left Newport News. Some are already seasick. Hopefully the water will calm down and it won't be like this the whole trip.

It was a little surprising that we are making this trip alone, with no escort convoy in the submarine-infested waters of the Atlantic. Those German U-boats make it hard on Allied ships. It's a big victory for them if they can hit a troop ship before the soldiers ever make it to battle.

The Anderson is a new troop transport. The sailors say that it can out run the U-boats and their torpedoes. That's why we don't have destroyer protection. I hope they are right. I suppose we will find out.

I went to a Christmas Eve prayer service tonight that some of the Protestant chaplains put together. It's getting late, but I can't sleep. It is crowded and there is too much going on in my mind. That is why I am writing tonight. When I saw Geraldine in Washington last month, she gave me this notebook and suggested I keep a journal. This is the first time I've written in it, but I think I will give it a try.

U.S. Army troops preparing to leave for overseas during World War II at the Hampton Roads Port of Embarkation in Newport News, VA .

U.S. Army Signal Corp photographs

25 Dec 1943

Christmas Day at sea.   The ocean is calmer today.   It's hard not to miss home.   I guess I miss Momma most of all, just like I did last Christmas.   I keep thinking of Mildred too.   Momma always liked Mildred.   I don't second guess myself much, but the more I am away from her, the more I wonder if I made the right decision about not asking her to marry me yet.   But it wouldn't be fair to her for us to get married and then me ship overseas.   I could get killed.   Just not the smart thing for either of us, but I do miss that girl.   I just have to hope & pray that God brings me through whatever lies ahead and she is still there when I get back.

CHAPTER THREE
A DAY OF LOSS

July 30, 1942

Yesterday, B.B. Darnell had turned 21 years old, sitting at his mother's bedside.   She had been in poor health for many years – the result of a bout with rheumatic fever when she was a child that had damaged her heart.   This morning, at 42 years of age, she had passed away.   B.B.'s grief was like nothing he had ever experienced before.   He knew he would never get over losing her. His mother was his greatest confidant and encourager.   His biggest supporter.   The person he could share everything with. Now she was gone.

Just a couple of months earlier, she was there when he received his college degree from Alabama Polytechnic University (API) and was commissioned as a second lieutenant in the United States Army Field Artillery Reserve.   Even knowing he was headed to war, it was one of his happiest moments as his parents watched him graduate and become an officer.   His mother was so proud of him that day as she pinned his Second Lieutenant bars on him.

B.B. always gave his parents reasons to be proud.   That was just who he was. Even as a youngster, B.B. worked hard to excel in everything he did, whether it was school, farming, work, or sports. He was raised that way - the result of having an educated,

11

demanding, but fair father who was a teacher and farmer; and a mother who was loving & attentive with a great sense of humor and even greater faith in God.

Home to B.B. was the Lee County, Alabama, farm on which he was born and where he grew up.   He was the middle child born to Marshall & Ocie Darnell.   His brother Carl was one year older and sister Geraldine was two years younger.

As Marshall left the room to go outside, Carl's wife Frances and Marshall's sister Flossie tried to comfort Ocie's grieving children.

"I'm going to call Mildred and see if she can come over," Frances said as she hugged B.B.   "That would be good," he responded softly.

Mildred Moore was a friend of Geraldine & Frances, who lived about 10 miles away near Auburn. B.B. first met her when he was 13 years old at one of the parties that some of the parents in the rural area would have from time to time for the children.   As she became closer friends with his sister, Mildred & B.B. were around each other more and more.   In their late teens, their romantic interest in each other grew as well.   She and Frances were especially close to Ocie, who encouraged both the girls in their relationships with her boys.   Even though B.B. had dated other girls, Mildred was the one person besides his mother who it was always easy to talk with.   She was one of his closest friends, and at this time of loss, he needed to have her near.

"That would be real good," B.B. said again quietly.

Marshall & Ocie Darnell   *B.B. Darnell with his mother, Ocie, 1941*

B.B., Carl, and Geraldine Darnell in the late 1930s

Mildred Moore

Alabama Polytechnic Institute ROTC Battery A at Ft Benning, GA, 1941, with B.B. Darnell on the front row.

CHAPTER FOUR
CROSSING THE ATLANTIC

25 Dec 1943

First day at sea in a crowded troop ship is not the best way to spend Christmas, but at least we're not getting shot at yet. And they did feed us turkey for Christmas dinner. I even thought we were going to have sweet potato pie, but it turned out to be pumpkin. It was a good Christmas dinner though.

The enlisted men eat standing up on the ship. They go through a line with their mess kit and then stand while eating at a long stainless steel table with a lip on it. I suppose the lip is to keep the mess kit from sliding off during heavy seas. The officers' situation is a little better as we eat together in a dining room where we get to sit down.

One thing I noticed right off as we were at sea was that there was a lot of garbage and oil floating in the water off shore. I guess this is from all the ships coming & going across the Atlantic during wartime. While I tried not to think of it – some of the debris could have been from ships that had been hit by Nazi U-boats. Not exactly what I thought the water would look like on my first time out in the deep blue Atlantic. We don't get much time on deck, so I won't see much anyway. It was cloudy, dreary, and misting rain when I was on deck earlier today.

The USS Anderson does move fast I suppose, but it is hard to tell

15

because we are zig-zagging our way along. The sailors say it makes it harder for any subs looking for us. Looking behind us, the wake is one long series of Zs. Has to take twice as long as a straight route.

This morning we had our first lifeboat drill. We are to have them every day at 1000 hours. When the bell rings we head up to the deck for the "Abandon Ship" drill. We are supposed to wear our lifejacket at all times except when sleeping – and then you have to keep it close to you. The best thing about the drill is that it gets the men out on the deck for a little bit before they have to go back down below. They don't get to walk around much on the deck, but pretty much have to stand in the assigned place. We have all been warned that if anyone falls overboard they would be left behind.

26 Dec 1943

This trip on the Anderson makes me glad I'm not in the Navy. A lot of the boys have been seasick, and while I've felt queasy at times, I haven't thrown up – yet.

The crew tells us this is the second troop transport voyage the Anderson has made. On the first one, they ran into a hurricane with winds more than 100 mph. I hope we don't have any of that kind of weather.

The crew doesn't know where we are going either. They said that, for security reasons, the captain opens his orders only when the ship is safely at sea, so the crew doesn't know yet. They did tell us that the last trip they made was to Casablanca though.

The sleeping arrangements are crowded I'm in a room with 12 other junior officers. We sleep in 3-tier bunks that are pretty close, but it is a better arrangement than the enlisted men have. They have canvas bunks/hammocks hanging one on top of the other from a bunch of steel pipes. All the way from the floor to the ceiling. Each hammock is about two feet wide and six feet long. They are hung so close that if you try to roll over or raise your knees, you are going to bump somebody. The smell is bad – 5000 men crammed in this ship, many throwing up. I think all have gas – whew. Plus there are lots of snorers.

The Battalion commander told us about the conditions to expect on the ship, but it was hard to imagine. He told us to keep the men busy and there will be less seasickness, but it is hard to keep them busy when everything is so confined. Most occupy their time by playing cards.

Troop ship quarters were cramped. National Archives photo

27 Dec 1943

Christmas dinner was good, but now the boys are complaining about the food. I guess it wouldn't be the army if people weren't complaining about something. The enlisted men are fed in pretty much continuous shifts, two meals a day. No matter what they feed us, it seems we get powdered eggs and powdered potatoes with it. Doesn't seem that bad to me, but it gives them something to complain about.

It is a peculiar feeling to know that after more than a year of full-time soldiering in preparation for war, we are finally headed toward it – wherever that might be.

28 Dec 1943

Scuttlebutt is that if we were headed to the Pacific, we would be seeing islands & shorelines by now headed to the Panama Canal. No land near us at all. I really never thought we were headed to the Pacific, based on our training. Plus, if we were, you would think that they would have shipped us out from southern California while we were there, instead of sending us back east. But I've learned, you can never underestimate the Army's ability to do something that doesn't make sense. I think most of the guys are relieved that we are not going to the Pacific Theater, but now the question is – where are we going? England, Italy, or North Africa?

Most of the news about the fighting in Europe has been pretty good. Maybe the Germans will surrender before we ever have to fight.

Life on a ship is one big greasy, oily place. Our uniforms are filthy from the grease which covers all the exposed machinery of the ship. The life jackets we were given were greasy when we got them. Seems like there is a thin skim of oily dirt covering all the floors. And when we can take a shower, the water is cold seawater. Soap doesn't do much good with seawater.

The smell below is getting foul. We have to stay below the deck except for the lifeboat drills. Time above deck is limited for us because we have to stay out of the way of the sailors. It can get pretty dull below deck.

Some of the soldiers were selected to help the sailors with the anti-aircraft deck guns. Those guys get to spend more time on deck each day. It's a good assignment. There are four big 5" double guns, sixteen of the 1.1" guns, and twenty 20mm guns.

The seagulls who followed us out to sea have long since disappeared. Now the times we are up on deck the scenery is pretty much the same all the time, except for an occasional school of porpoises.

30 Dec 1943

The ocean was really rough yesterday. Lots of boys got sick. It's bad because if you're in your hammock and the boy above you gets seasick, sometimes they throw up there and the guys below him get it. We keep cleaning details going, but the whole area below stinks. When it gets rough like that, about all you can do is lay in your bunk and try to ride it out.

Luckily the water is calmer today. When the weather is decent like today, I wish I could just stay up on deck.

We got our third and final typhus shot today. We got the other two at Ft. Henry when preparing for embarkation. The typhus shot is one of the most painful ones – it burns a lot like the anti-tetanus they gave us. But we're glad to get it because we have heard there is a typhoid epidemic in Italy and the shots are keeping our soldiers there from getting it.

We keep up with what is going on in the world with two radio broadcast each day – the BBC in the morning and an American news broadcast in the afternoon. Russians are making progress against the Germans on the eastern front and the British and American troops are moving slowly in southern Italy.

The news from the Pacific doesn't sound as good as the Marines are trying to get a foothold. I wonder where Carl is right now. I hope he is okay. Knowing him, he is right in the middle of whatever is going on – good or bad.

31 Dec 1943

New Year's Eve and we're headed to war. Makes everyone apprehensive about what 1944 holds for us. 1943 was sure different for me – thanks to the Army travel service! Before the Army I had never been out of Alabama, except that one time a group of us took the train over to Columbus for the Georgia game. In the last year, Uncle Sam has given me a tour of some of his "finest" facilities in Oklahoma, Mississippi, Louisiana, North Carolina, New Jersey, California, and Virginia. And here I am now, on a ship headed into 1944 and who knows where.

We are all tired of this ship. We've had pretty good weather overall. I read my Bible every night. A lot of the guys do. There are good boys with me here, and several from the South who grew up on farms. That makes it easier.

There is some big band music playing over the ship's loudspeakers tonight, making everybody think of New Year's Eve parties at home. Lots of talk of home and girls. I wonder what Mildred is doing tonight.

1 Jan 1944

Happy New Year.   Sitting around the table on New Year's Day in Alabama with everybody seems like decades ago.   I do miss home. A lot of the boys here got married or engaged right before leaving.   But that just didn't seem right for Mildred and me – to do that and then leave.   Besides, we agreed not to rush into anything. This war has turned everything upside down for folks. So we said we would write, see others if we want, and if we are meant to be together, then it will happen.

Looks like we are headed to North Africa.   Hopefully this will be over soon.   Sounds like the Germans aren't doing so well in southern Italy.   Maybe this time next year, I will be home with everybody.

My unit, the 328th FA, starts this New Year with 488 Enlisted Men, 2 Warrant Officers and 30 Officers on the high seas, headed for combat.

The USS General A.E. Anderson troop ship during World War II

21

CHAPTER FIVE
TRAINING FOR WAR

September 1, 1942

Five weeks after his mother's death, Second Lieutenant B.B. Darnell stepped off the bus at the Field Artillery Training & Replacement Depot at Ft. Bragg, NC. Lt. Darnell was no longer in the Army Reserve, but was now on active duty. With his arrival at Ft. Bragg, he was joining hundreds of other new artillerymen training at the base. The camp had constructed extensive artillery ranges during World War I and they were being put to good use in the summer and fall of 1942.

Full time Army life was an adjustment for the quiet young soldier from rural Alabama, particularly at Ft. Bragg. The camp's population had grown from 5500 soldiers in 1940 to almost 100,000 in late 1942. It was like being in a big city and everything seemed like mass confusion. New soldiers were coming and going daily as they were being trained, processed and sent to units as replacements.

After a month of training at Ft. Bragg, Second Lieutenant Darnell received his orders to attend Field Artillery School in Ft. Sill, OK. Until that time B.B. Darnell had hardly been out of Alabama, much less west of the Mississippi. The U.S. Army was changing all of that.

In early October, Darnell boarded a train with several other artillerymen for the journey west to Lawton, Oklahoma. The Army had opened a Field Artillery Officer Candidate School (OCS) at Fort Sill to help meet the need for leaders in the rapidly expanding Army. The OCS trained the men who came out of ROTC in college or had been chosen out of the ranks of the enlisted men to become officers. It was tough, intensive training that produced young officers that became known as "90 Day Wonders" amongst the Army veterans.

The 12 week course was demanding. The physical challenges, the leadership training, as well as the theoretical and practical coursework of modern artillery was designed to push the candidates to their limits. Some washed out. It was challenging, but young Lt. Darnell actually enjoyed the math calculations, trigonometry, and map reading required to become a field artillery officer. His Auburn ROTC training had prepared him well.

*Lt. B.B. Darnell, at Ft. Sill, OK,
for Field Artillery School,
December, 1943*

After completion of Field Artillery School, Lt. Darnell received his unit assignment. On February 1, 1943, he reported to Camp Shelby Mississippi to the newly activated 85th Infantry Division, 328th Field Artillery as an Assistant Battery Executive Officer.

Camp Shelby was a sprawling base in southern Mississippi that used over a thousand square miles for training thousands of troops. Like most Army training bases at the time, it was bustling with activity as it rapidly expanded to handle the needs of the wartime Army. Soldiers were housed in tents and in tar paper and wood frame "hutments". As he settled into his hutment, Darnell was glad to be back in the South with warmer weather.

He had no idea that just a few days earlier, halfway around the world, in Casablanca, Morocco, Allied leaders had made the decision to launch an invasion against the German Armies on the mainland of Europe, specifically in Italy. His new unit, the 85th Division, known as "The Custermen", would be the outfit with which Darnell would enter and fight in that assault.

Cover of pamphlet given to new members of the 85th Division

25

When Lt. Darnell arrived at Camp Shelby, he was immediately immersed in the intensive training underway for the men of the 85th. Road marches of up to 25 miles with full packs were commonplace. Daily physical training was ongoing and strenuous. Battalion and division-level field maneuvers were conducted in nearby DeSoto National Forest.

After two months of this type of training at Camp Shelby, Lt. Darnell moved, along with the rest of the 85th Division, to a wooded rural area near Leesville, Louisiana, for corps maneuvers. These maneuvers included extensive mock combat exercises with other divisions and units. In the swampy woodlands the men dealt with mosquitos, chiggers, ticks, and snakes as their training continued. For eight weeks, the Custermen lived outside in the Louisiana woods, sleeping on the ground and experiencing combat situations to a degree they had not yet been exposed.

At the end of May, the Division left the woods of Louisiana for a new type of training environment. One that would be vastly different from any they had experienced. With the war in North Africa continuing, there was a demand for troops with desert combat experience. The 85th loaded onto trains and headed westward for desert training at Camp Pilot Knob, eleven miles west of Yuma, AZ, in the Mojave Desert of southern California.

In the heat of the summer of 1943, the training days were long and difficult. The 85th was the only division at that time to ever complete desert warfare training at this location in the full heat of the summer months. Daytime temperatures could reach in excess of 120 degrees. The men were unaccustomed to desert life, many suffering heat prostration, cramps, and dehydration. All soldiers were required to take salt tablets daily. While the heat was dangerous, the wind could make life miserable as well. The fine sandy soil and frequent sandstorms left camps & equipment in disarray and coated everything with dirt and sand. The extreme environment made all training exercises dangerous, but prepared the men for the difficult duties ahead of them.

Desert Training Center in California in 1942

On July 2, 1943, while Lt. Darnell was training in this strange and harsh environment, his father remarried. By this time, his brother Carl had been shipped overseas and was fighting in the Pacific with the Marine Corps. His sister Geraldine had moved to Washington, D.C., and was working in the secretarial pool at the Pentagon. Mildred was living in Opelika where she was employed as a telephone operator. In the course of a year he had lost his mother, his father had married someone he did not know, and his family and friends were scattered everywhere. His entire life had been turned upside down. The world was at war and he was in the United States Army preparing to join the conflict.

Lt. Darnell's next step toward that war occurred in early October, 1943. The 85th Division, boarded trains again. This time for the cross country trip to their new post in Ft. Dix, NJ.   The four day transcontinental journey gave the men who had trained so hard a brief rest and a panorama of the United States. From the heat of the Mojave, through the sparse southwest, the plains of Kansas, the farmland of the Midwest, to the bustle of Chicago's busy rail yard their trains rolled eastward. From there, across the pleasant-looking farms of Ohio and rolling hillsides of Pennsylvania and into the brisk, refreshing autumn weather of New Jersey, they arrived at Ft. Dix different men than when they first reported to Camp Shelby.

As they settled in their new station at Ft. Dix, brief furloughs were granted. Old and worn equipment and supplies were traded in for new. A regimen of paperwork and inoculations began as they continued to train. Men were told to get their affairs in order. At this time they were the most highly trained division in Army history. Everyone knew that their move to Ft. Dix was in preparation to be shipped somewhere overseas. Their time of war was near.

328th Field Artillery Officers (with Lt. Darnell on back row, center) Ft. Dix, NJ, late October 1943

B. B. Darnell's Training Tour of the U.S.
Notasulga, AL → Ft. Bragg, NC → Ft. Sill, OK → Camp Shelby, MS →
Leesville, LA → Camp Pilot Knob, CA → Ft. Dix, NJ → Ft. Patrick Henry, VA

Geraldine & B.B. Darnell in Washington, D.C., November 1943

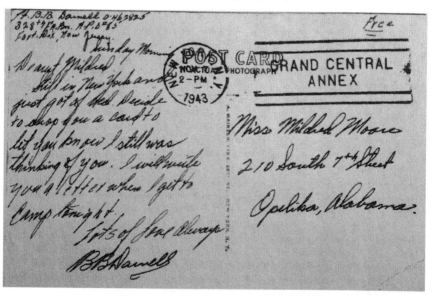

The only existing correspondence from B.B. to Mildred during World War II, a postcard written November 7, 1943, while B.B. was stationed at Ft. Dix, NJ.

CHAPTER SIX
NORTH AFRICA

2 Jan 1944

Finally back on land.   After waiting for a minesweeper to makes sure the channel was clear, we docked in Casablanca early this morning.   I never imagined in my life, I would travel to Africa, and yet here I am tonight in Morocco in northern Africa.   The voyage made walking on land again a little different, but it didn't take long to adjust!   I was glad to get off that boat.   I do believe it will take us all a little time to get back into shape though.   It was hard to get much exercise on the ship.

When we moored at the dock in Casablanca, standing at the rail of the ship looking down, I realized this place is much different than anywhere I had ever been.   Everywhere on the docks were beggars dressed in rags that looked like old, worn-out, croaker sacks.   Their hands out for anything a soldier would give them. These people looked worse off than anybody I had ever seen.   It seems the only English they knew was their plea of "Alms for the love of Allah".   We were advised to ignore them and their pleas, but it is hard to see people in that condition.   Even during the worst of the Depression, we were better off on the farm than these people...at least we had food.

But beyond the beggars, there was activity everywhere with American troops & dock workers.   Our ship was the first of the 85th Division to arrive here.   We disembarked the ship and were immediately loaded onto trucks with our gear and we were headed away from the docks by early afternoon.

We got brief glimpses of Casablanca as the trucks sped through the streets – dirty streets, dirty white buildings, more beggars, barefoot men with Turbans and white gowns, camels, men riding small donkeys, women covered head to toe walking behind their husbands. That was about all we saw of the city, and that suited me just fine.

Tonight we are a few miles outside of Casablanca in Camp Don B. Passage. The camp is named after the first American soldier killed in the invasion of North Africa. It is pretty bare bones, but the countryside around us is surprisingly green and pretty. It's getting cold here tonight. We are in tents with wooden floors, so it is better than being outside.

My first night in a foreign country. My senses were overloaded as I took in the sights, the different countryside, the different languages, the smells, the sounds, and the people that are so different from home. I have no idea what is next. It is scary, but exciting in a way.

7 Jan 1944

We've been busy getting everything squared away here. After a couple of days at Camp Passage, we loaded onto old French World War I rail cars called "40 or 8" – which means 40 men or 8 donkeys. So we loaded up like cattle and headed out of the Casablanca area into the Atlas Mountains in Algiers. The trains rocked and swayed worse than the ship as we were going through the mountains. The scenery was something else, but the long, smoked filled tunnels made us hope for a short trip. Even with that, though, it is hard not to be amazed by God's creation. This is so different from the countryside I'm used to.

We finally arrived at a place called St. Denis-du-Sig, unloaded and then began a two mile hike to our camp. It was a big, open area surrounded by barbed wire. We found out it used to be a POW camp. We were given straw pallets to sleep on. Not many amenities here.

10 Jan 1944

Rumor is that this is to be our home for a few weeks as we began training for mountain warfare and getting back into shape after the ship voyage. This is a lot different than the training in the woods & swamps of Louisiana or the flat desert training in California. We have a lot to learn. The boys are all pretty sure we are going to Italy eventually, but we don't know when or where. Lots of mountains in Italy though, so we have to learn about mountain fighting. I have already discovered that climbing through these mountains, I use a whole new set of leg & back muscles I didn't even know I had.

This is a remote area, but there are always Arab men around. They follow us everywhere. It is a little un-nerving the way they follow you around. Everywhere you go, 4-5 are watching you. You get the feeling that if they caught you alone in the dark, you would be robbed and killed. Apparently, they consider all the American soldiers rich and their religion doesn't like Christians in their country. Because of that, we don't go anywhere alone.

12 Jan 1944

Don't know if I will ever get used to these warm days and the intense cold at nights, but I think we are getting a little better acclimated. The desert training we did in the Mojave back in the States was during the summer, so it got hotter during the day, but we didn't freeze at night.

A few nights ago, a couple of us thought we had a great idea and made our bed in the back of the two-ton trucks thinking that would be warmer than the ground. We learned differently. The cold wind blowing under that wooden truck bed was a lot colder than the ground! About 1 am, we finally gave it up and got back on the ground with our straw pallets. Lesson learned.

16 Jan 1944

Food here isn't bad.   When we aren't training on the move, we have hot meals at the mess tent.   The cooks do okay – sometimes it's good and sometimes it's...well, its hot food. If we're out in the field on the move, we have C rations, although in the last few days we've started getting more K rations.

Got a letter from Carl today. He is somewhere in the Pacific. Any details have been blacked out, but it sounds like he is okay. I wish he hadn't joined the Marine Corps. He has a wife and daughter. He knew I was going to end up going since I was in ROTC. But I know how Carl is. Even Daddy couldn't talk him out of it.

Lt. Darnell with mess kit on the chow line in North Africa.

Photo courtesy of Bill Dempsey, son of Capt. William Dempsey

2 Feb 1944

Yesterday we moved from the mountains to the Invasion Training Center at Port Aux Poules, Algeria, on the Mediterranean coast. I knew we hadn't finished our mountain training, so this was a surprise. Looks like we are going to be doing amphibious training.   This may mean we are headed to the beachhead at Anzio just south of Rome. The Germans have had some of the Fifth Army boys pinned down there for a couple of weeks.

11 Feb 1944

Got a letter from Aunt Flossie yesterday.   It's always good to hear from someone back home.   She says things are good there. Geraldine got home from Washington for a few days.   Sounds like Carol is growing like a weed.   I will write back to her tomorrow when I have more time.

16 Feb 1944

This amphibious landing training is proving to be the most dangerous we've been through.   Rough seas and difficulty in maneuvering the landing craft are causing all kinds of problems. Along the shore, undercurrents have cut away deep holes.   On several occasions, the LCVP's hit sand bars, and as the soldiers moved out of the landing craft, some plunged into these holes over their heads.   4 boys from the 339th Infantry were lost when the ramp on their LCVP came down out in the rough, deeper water off the coast in the dark one morning.   Everybody on board went into the cold water.   We were lucky we didn't lose more.   Others have been lost in other incidents.

Rumors are rampant that the division is slated to reinforce the surrounded IV Corps Fifth Army units within the beach head at Anzio.   This will be tough duty.   This training has been dangerous enough, but an amphibious landing in battle – the casualties will be high.

27 Feb 1944

Maybe we aren't headed to Anzio after all.   After the last 3 weeks of training on the coast, we are back in the mountains at St. Denis-du-Sig, working on our mountain combat training again. Who knows though?   One thing I have learned about being in the Army is to never count anything out.   After hearing stories of the fighting around Cassino, I'm not sure which would be worse – Anzio or Cassino. We still don't know where we're going or when, but I bet it won't be much longer till we move.

Food here is okay, at least we usually have hot food of some sort. Tonight we had a hot dog sliced up with peas, carrots, bread, and tea. I'm sure the cooks do the best they can with what they have. What they call sweet tea wouldn't pass for sweet tea at home.

11 Mar 1944

Something big is happening now. The 339th moved out suddenly 3 days ago, leaving the rest of the Division here in the mountains. Today, we got orders to prepare for a "movement by water." The anticipation and curiosity is about to get the best of all of us, but I guess we will know soon enough. Looks like we are headed to the coast near Oran, but after that, who knows?

13 Mar 1944

Today has had to be one of the hottest days we've had. But we had fried chicken for dinner! Not as good as momma's but it was one of the better meals we've had. Don't know how they got chicken here for us, but I know it wasn't dehydrated like the potatoes & gravy – it was real.

17 Mar 1944

We have been bivouacked on the coast near Oran now for about a week. We continue to train daily. We are all back in good shape – the mountain training took care of that. Everybody knows something is up and we're eager to find out what is happening.

I have to say that the Mediterranean Sea is beautiful. It is sandy and warm here, but we do get a little time to swim each day and I really enjoy that. We all know though, that the battles are across the Mediterranean and we will be there soon.

Being halfway around the world, it seems like such a long time since I was at home. So much has happened in the last few months.

Colonel Burton advising some of the men of the 328th FA that they were leaving North Africa to move into battle.
Photo courtesy of Bill Dempsey

Men of the 328th FA "packed and ready to go" at Oran on March 24, 1944, the day they left North Africa for Naples.
Photo courtesy of Bill Dempsey

24 Mar 1944

We are back on the water again. Earlier today the remainder of the Division loaded onto four ships and left as a convoy out of Oran. This trip we have a destroyer escort and a blimp overhead for aircraft protection. The sea is rough.

Right now I am sitting under deck on the USS Nightingale, packed in with everybody else. Not nearly as big of ship as the Anderson, but our journey shouldn't be as long.

No doubt we are headed to Italy and the good news is that, based on our preparation & equipment, we won't be doing an amphibious landing. That is an answered prayer for all of us. That was dangerous enough during the training without anyone shooting at us. It's crowded in here and is going to be hard to get any sleep. Just like when we crossed the Atlantic, access to the deck is restricted, so hopefully it won't take too long to get where we are going.

105mm howitzer crew in North Africa.
National Archives photo.

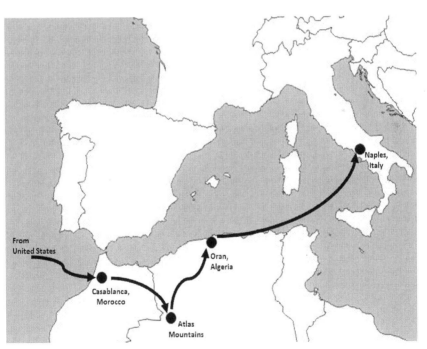

B.B. Darnell's Route to Italy

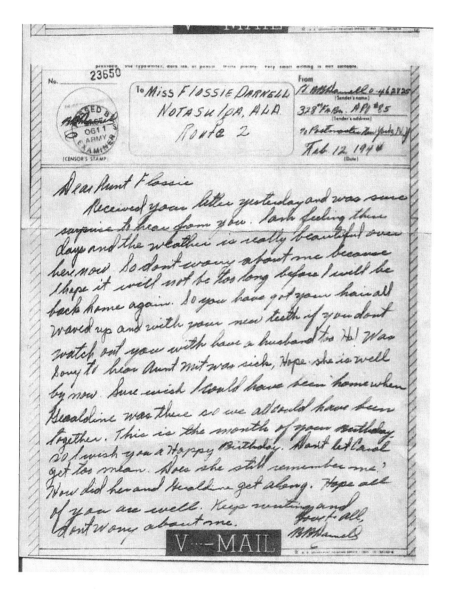

A copy of the V-Mail letter Lt. Darnell wrote to his Aunt Flossie on February 12, 1944. This is the only letter located from him during his time overseas.

CHAPTER SEVEN
ITALY

27 Mar 1944

We are anchored in the dock at Naples, Italy right now, preparing to disembark from the ships. Naples is in Allied hands now with the front about 40 miles north. It is a devastated looking city. Looks like whatever we didn't destroy with our bombing, the Nazis destroyed before they left. I don't see a single building along the waterfront that is standing without some damage. Hulls of sunken ships are visible everywhere in the harbor where the Germans tried to block the harbor.

As we entered the bay & harbor in Naples, we could see Mt. Vesuvius south of the town still smoking from its eruption a couple of weeks ago. First time I've ever seen a smoking volcano. They said when it erupted, it destroyed some American planes at the airfield south of here and covered everything with ash. You can still see soot & ash at places along the docks. Between the war and the volcano, these folks have had a rough time. Because of a typhus epidemic among the civilians, the Allies quarantined Naples in January until they could get it under control.

Looks like I'm about to enter my third foreign country in 3 months. The sooner I get back to Lee County, Alabama, the better as far as I'm concerned. This place gives me a different feeling. It is obvious we are now in an active theater of war. I think all of us wonder if we are up to what lies ahead. The massive destruction in this place churns lots of emotions.

Mt Vesuvius' last major eruption occurred March 18-23, 1944. Lt. B.B. Darnell arrived in Naples on March 27. Allied jeeps are shown in the foreground as Vesuvius smokes behind them. National Archives photo.

28 Mar 1944

Tonight we are in bivouac in a training area north of Naples. Last night was a long night on the docks with the riggers unloading equipment while we tried to catch some sleep. This morning, we loaded into 2-1/2 ton trucks headed north out of the city. The air raid sirens and searchlights went on last night, but the German planes never showed. Apparently their nighttime bombing of Naples has slowed some, but it is still a regular occurrence.

The smell of Naples was bad. Trash & rubble everywhere and open sewage in the streets. The people there are literally starving. Drinking water is scarce and our K & C rations seemed to be the only source of food around. Some of the Italians helping us load our supplies into the trucks were given some C rations and they acted like we had given them a million dollars. These folks have had it rough – their homes & businesses destroyed and their families starving. They are still alive, but it is a tough way to live. During my short time out of the U.S., I've seen more poor, starving people than I ever knew existed.

As we moved out of the city, it was plain to see that Italy is a beautiful country...and war has disfigured her beauty.

American troops in trucks making their way through Naples.
National Archives photo

30 Mar 1944

We aren't at the front yet, but we are close. We are north of Naples, training in preparation to enter the line. Some of the boys in 339th are already there, but we're attached to the 337th Infantry right now. Near Mt. Massico, in a training area northeast of Sant' Angelo.

We have hot meals here – actually better than I expected. We also get a pack of cigarettes, two pieces of chewing gum, and a pack of lifesavers each day. I'm glad I don't smoke because the cigarettes come in handy for trade.

Mt. Massico (north of Naples) where 328th Field Artillery trained prior to entering battle in April 1944. Photograph taken in 2014

2 Apr 1944

Life in Italy is different.   In the little village here we saw a goat herder with his goats going through the street.   As he moved along, women would come out of their houses with a pan or a jug and the herder would stop and milk a goat into the woman's pan. She would pay him and he would move on down the street.   Now that is fresh milk.

You could also see women along the street combing their children's hair with fine tooth combs.   They were combing the lice out. They would then drop the lice in olive oil in a saucer to kill them.

In our camp here, someone built a big ten-holer outhouse facility, right out in the open for us to use. It doesn't have any sides, but at least it has a roof. Can't be shy in the Army.

We hear the constant rumblings of artillery to the north of us. We are out of range here.   I'm working with the infantry as a FO.   We continue to work on fire missions, movement, and communications.

5 Apr 1944

Every morning about 4 AM the area farmers go to work in their big two-wheeled carts.   Seems like none of them have two donkeys, or two ox, or two horses – so the carts are always pulled by a mixed pair.   This morning, one came by that was pulled by an ox and a skinny donkey.   The father in the front driving, with the mother and two small children in the back.   The mother was singing some Italian song as they made their way down the road.   Reminded me of when I was little and Momma used to sing to me.

8 Apr 1944

Been a busy week.   Our training has gotten a lot more serious, a lot more intense.   Everybody is alert and focused now.   This close to the front, everything changes.   We continue to train in mountain warfare, while also training for attacking villages, and safe stream crossings. These are good boys I'm here with.   From all over the country – places I've never heard of, but all good boys.   I'm lucky that there are some other boys from the South here with me - makes it a little easier.

I've seen my first olive trees.   Daddy would like to see those and the way they grow them.   Lots of fig trees too and grapes.   And they have these pine trees that look like umbrellas. Without a war, this would be beautiful countryside.   We aren't far from the Mediterranean – probably just a couple of miles.   You can see its shimmering waters as you move on higher ground. Unfortunately, we don't have time to enjoy it.

It was good to get another letter from Mildred today.   I miss that girl.   It's been too long since we've sat in the porch swing and just talked.   I miss her laugh, the sound of her voice.   Sounds like things are going okay for her in Opelika, even with the rationing and shortages back home. It is good to hear from her. What I wouldn't give to hold her hand right now. I really miss her.

9 Apr 1944

It is Easter Sunday. There was an Easter Service this morning for everybody.

Looks like the Division will began moving into frontline positions tomorrow. Different units of the Division will occupy an area from the Tyrrhenian coastline east of Scauri westward to just north of Minturno. The Germans are dug in fortifications in the mountains north of Minturno along a line they call the Gustav Line. They hold all the terrain advantages. About 70 miles north of that is Rome, which is the ultimate prize once we jump off.

We've been warned that the Germans send out patrols regularly to try to take prisoners for the purpose of obtaining information. Tonight we talked to the men about this in preparation for moving. If captured you are required to give only 3 facts: your name, your rank, and your Army serial number. It is best not to talk about anything, don't try to fake stories, and try to destroy any papers you have on you – even personal letters.

CHAPTER EIGHT
DANGEROUS DUTY

April 1 1944

"Darnell, you're set to start FO duty with 2nd Battalion."

With that assignment from his Battery Commander, Second Lieutenant B.B. Darnell embarked on the most dangerous seven months of his life.

Charlie Battery had set up near Mt. Massico for final preparation to enter the front line north of Naples. They had been in Italy for four days.

"You need to report to the CO there for assignment with a rifle company," Lt. William Dempsey continued. "You will rotate in and out with them for the next few weeks."

Darnell knew the assignment was coming. All new officers who attended Field Artillery School in Ft. Sill, were trained in all aspects of field artillery, including forward observation. He had learned at Ft. Sill that FO duty normally went to the younger officers. While it was an important job, assignment as a forward observer was not a desirable job.

As he left the CO's tent, the memorized description of the duties of a forward observer ran through Lt. Darnell's mind:

"The Forward Observer directs the fire of the artillery unit from a forward position. He observes shell bursts and adjusts fire by forward observation or computation methods; he consults with commanders of supported units in determination of appropriate artillery targets, normal barrage, and zones of defense; he trains personnel in procedures of artillery operation; he organizes observation posts; he sets up and maintains communication systems."

Darnell knew he could handle the described duties. He had done it over and over again during their months of training in the U.S. and North Africa. But he had never done it in real battle, facing an enemy trying to kill him.

In combat, the field artillery has two ways to locate its targets – unobserved fire, which is basically firing blindly to a location, or observed fire, which is far more effective. The forward observer is the key to effective observed fire, but to be able to do the job, the FO has to be at the front line, oftentimes in front of the troops he is supporting. Duty as an observer usually occurred on a rotating basis among the officers in a battery, going out on the front line for days at a time. When the battle situation was more active, an observer or observation team may stay with a particular infantry unit for extended periods of time.

The configuration of artillery forward observation on the ground during the war in Italy varied as the situations changed. When possible, the forward observation was done by a team consisting

48

of 4-5 men. The team would be led by a lieutenant, with a sergeant, a radio operator, and a rifleman or two. Each member of the team would have the knowledge of the radio procedure and reading the grid for fire detection to complete the mission if necessary. The team could be a fixed position at the front or moving with an infantry unit in battle.

Other times, the FO team could consist of just the forward observer and a radioman. Sometimes it was solitary duty for one observer.

Forward Observers accompanied infantrymen into combat, crawled into no-man's land, and climbed hills and ridges, trying to be invisible in order to find their targets. They had to be close enough to see and observe enemy actions, for the purpose of giving fire support whenever and where ever needed. It was dangerous duty. Beyond the usual perils of ground combat, FOs were specially targeted by the enemy because of their crucial role in directing artillery fire. They were regularly the focus of unwanted attention by the enemy. Their life expectancy in those situations was estimated at two weeks.

A 1944 U.S. Army publication declared that in ground combat, "The forward observer is potentially the most powerful individual in the forward area."

On April Fool's Day, 1944, Lt. Darnell began this dangerous duty. For seven months, until he was wounded on October 12, 1944, his forward observer responsibilities put him on the front of infantry assaults as the Allied Army moved north through Italy.

U.S. Army Artillery Forward Observer from the 34th Infantry Division in the central Apennine Mountains of Italy.
National Archives photo

CHAPTER NINE
INTO THE LINE

12 Apr 1944

We entered the front line in an area called Cava di Calcare last night around midnight, near an old limestone rock quarry area just east of Minturno. We have been setting up the 105's and began registering them today.

We left the bivouac area loaded into the trucks. The Army has been generous in outfitting us, but it's so much, you wonder if you can even move with it all. Overcoat, raincoat, field jacket, long underwear, ODs, and combat suit, plus 2 blankets, mess kit, weapons, and other equipment. I know we will need it all, but it almost makes you feel like you can't move.

Last night we rode in the trucks for several miles with the lights on, then the drivers had to turn all the lights off as we continued. We realized at that moment, that we were in the combat area and our movements could be watched by the enemy. It was pitch black and the dirt road was narrow and muddy. I don't know how the drivers could even see where they were going. They had to stay right on the bumper of the truck in front of them.

When the trucks went as far as they could, we unloaded and organized everybody to go on foot the rest of the way. One behind the other, we had to stay on the slippery, muddy road because the fields on each side had been mined. Everybody was tense. It was a long, sloppy walk, in the Italian mud, but we made it to the line and dug in with the soldiers who we were there to relieve. Last night was a long, tiring night without much sleep. Probably going to be a lot of them ahead.

2014 photo showing the Cava di Calcare area east of Minturno where Lt. Darnell first entered battle in 1944.

13 Apr 1944

Saw my first dead German soldier near here today.   Not sure what killed him because I couldn't see any wounds. He was laying off the road a little, on his back.   Other than his stiff legs and arms sticking out awkwardly, you might have thought he was asleep.   His boots were gone.   The Italian civilians take the shoes off of any dead body they run across.   The people here don't have the bare necessities, especially shoes.   We didn't get too close to the body because we have been warned that they are sometimes booby-trapped.

The last couple of days, the gun crews have been busy getting ammunition ready and improving communication.   Guns are registered and fired a few rounds today.

15 Apr 1944

We are engaged with the enemy every day now. We are well trained, but nothing can prepare you for this. Shell fire is a frightening experience when it is coming toward you. In your hole, your heart is pounding and you imagine the whistling shells are looking just for you. Loud doesn't begin to describe the constant thunder from the German guns and our guns all going at the same time.

The 328th is attached to the 337th Infantry right now. I am working as an FO with them. We have taken over a portion of the front about 2 ½ miles long along the line. It is a lot of area to cover. I am calling in fire constantly against enemy movements and artillery positions. Orders are that we should fire 5 rounds for every German shell fired at us. Apparently we have an advantage in that respect and that makes it a lot easier on our infantry. Out constant shelling keeps the Germans in their dugouts during the day and forces them to do all their movement after dark. The noise from the shelling, both ours and theirs, is hard to get used to. It seems like it is all the time. From what we've been told, the German units we are facing have fought in France and Stalingrad. They are tough and battle hardened while we are all new to combat. But we are fresh and well-trained.

Just a little snow is still visible high on the mountains in the distance, but the valleys & hills are greening up with spring. Budding olive trees, orchards, and vineyards cover the hillsides with new life, as death is happening around us. If a man didn't have faith in God, I don't know how he could get through this.

18 Apr 1944

The Germans fired some propaganda leaflet shells near us today. Most of the boys got a laugh out of reading the pamphlets – telling us how bad the war is going for the Allies, that our leaders are lying to us, and that the only way we will ever see our families again is to surrender. These shells make a different noise when they are coming in – sort of a twang – and then they explode in the air and the paper floats down. I've heard we do the same thing, but no one in the 328ᵗʰ has fired any leaflet missions yet.

We've learned a lot about safe shelter here. Even though they look good, these abandoned farm houses you see here aren't safe. The Germans have been in position long enough to register those houses with their artillery. One or two rounds will kill everyone inside. It's much better to sleep outside, below ground level in a foxhole or slit trench. The slit trench is best. A couple of soldiers can dig it pretty quick. They are supposed to be 5' deep, 3' wide, and 7' long, shaped like an "L". The angle gives you somewhere to go if a grenade lands in the trench. We try to cover part of the top of the hole as well to give some protection from air burst. You have to have a good dugout.

21 Apr 1944

Yesterday, I took my forward observer party forward to a crest of a hill near the enemy lines so we could establish a better observation post. We are fairly exposed and they are shelling us constantly, day & night, but it gives us a better vantage point to direct fire on the enemy installations. From this point, I can see Castellonorato on a hill across the valley to my right, the entire valley below me, and the Mediterranean Sea on my left. It is a great vantage point, but unfortunately the Germans know we are here. We will stay here until relieved.

We've got a good dugout here. Whenever we stop anywhere, we dig holes. We sleep & eat in these holes. Daddy told me if I didn't go to college, I might end up digging ditches. Well, I've used a shovel more in the last month than I have in a long time – so much for that advice.

25 Apr 1944

Still at the forward OP. Last night 2 men in the C firing battery were killed by enemy shelling. There were 5 casualties in B Battery as the Germans continue to shell the firing positions. The enemy is entrenched in the high areas and have direct observation into both our forward and rear areas. Not a good situation for us to be in. Everywhere we go, it seems the Germans are dug in on the high ground. They have had lots of time to get ready for us.

When we set up a FO post, we have to string wires for communication as we move forward. The wires are just strung along the ground. The wires are constantly being cut by enemy fire. Repairing the wire is a dangerous job. We use radios when we can, especially if we're on the move, but the telephone is more reliable, especially in a fixed position like this.

27 Apr 1944

Last night we were relieved from the forward OP where we had been for the last 6 days. It was rough up there, but we all made it back. Glad to be out of there, but we continue to draw fire down here as well. It seems that there is no place safe from artillery fire, but we aren't as exposed here as we were in the O.P.

*I found some hay and have been able to line my hole with it –
anything to make it a little more comfortable.   Helps to keep
things dry and makes everything better.   Keeping things dry
makes life here easier – especially dry socks.   The Army does
have good wool socks.   I've learned to always have two pair.
When we are on the move I wear one and if they get wet, I take
them off & put on the dry ones. Dry socks are more valuable than
gold here.*

2 May 1944

*Back at the battery after 3 days at the forward OP.   The Germans
have set up defenses that are going to be hard to deal with.
Beyond the no-man's land valley there are mine fields and
barbed wire.   Then their well-prepared positions on the reverse
slopes that cover the crests of the hills with interlocking fields of
machine gun fire.   And beyond that are their higher positions on
the ridges where their artillery is placed from which they have
been firing at us.   They are well placed and waiting for us.*

*Right now I'm with C Battery, firing regularly.   The Battery is
doing a good job.   Things going on everywhere and all men
doing their part.   With better weather now, I believe things will
be breaking fast soon.*

*It's peculiar how soon you learn to discern the sounds of battle. I
suppose it is a self-preservation mechanism.   As loud as things
can be sometimes, you learn to hear some things automatically,
like the "whoop" of a mortar that lets you know one is coming in,
or the sound of a particular gun. It becomes second nature.*

*Glad to have that little Bible they gave us.   I keep Mildred's
picture in the front of it.   I try to read it every day.*

3 May 1944

Last night I was ordered on a mission with infantry patrol to get information about German positions, preferably by capturing some German soldiers. My first patrol of this type. I think it is a little unusual for artillery officers to go out with infantry on these patrols, but I spend more time out with the infantry boys than I do with artillery, so I guess the Captain just figured I was a part of them. Besides, it seems that they like to use the boys from the South for these patrols – most of us grew up in the woods hunting, so we are better sneaking around out there.

There were eight of us going out. We blackened our faces and tied all our gear we carried so it couldn't rattle. We emptied our pockets of all papers or personal letters in case we were captured. In the darkness, we moved out of our position near Minturno and into the valley below. We were about two miles behind German lines when we came up on 2 German soldiers sleeping in a cave. I guess they thought they would be safe there and were surprised when we woke them up. One of the boys with us could speak German, so that made it a lot easier with them. They surrendered to us, so we tied their hands, gagged them and began to move back to our lines with them. On the way back, the enemy spotted us and we came under heavy fire. I called in smoke to hide our movements as we ran back. It was dark, but the Germans had sent up flares that made things as bright as daylight. Then they started on us with automatic weapons fire & mortars. Their flares helped me too though, because I was able to locate their positions and bring artillery fire on them as we moved back to our line. It was a pretty hot situation, but all members of the patrol returned safely and we had two prisoners that could provide good information about German positions.

Area near Minturno that is likely where Lt. Darnell went on his first night patrol with infantry in April 1944. Photo taken in 2014.

6 May 1944

Sometimes we fire harassing missions trying to get the enemy mad enough to fire on us so we can locate their emplacements. Last night we took one gun from the battery out to another position to fire on the German positions hoping they would fire back. We try to maximize the flash on that gun so the Jerrys will be tempted. When they fire back at us, the FO would locate the enemy guns and then the entire battery would fire on them. While no one likes being on the harassing gun, last night it worked. We believe we silenced two of their guns with no casualties on our part.

9 May 1944

It is spring here and fields of red poppies are blooming. Everybody is tense, as we all know that a big offensive has been ordered – the push toward Rome through the Gustav Line. For the past couple of weeks, supplies of food, equipment, and ammo have been moved to the forward areas. More troops have been moved into place and things are a lot more crowded. This all has made it more important that our artillery keep the Germans dug in because one well-placed shell from their artillery could kill many of our guys. I've done lots of praying since getting to Italy, but the last few days, I believe everybody has. The biggest battles we will have lay ahead of us soon. Many of us could be injured or killed, but I think most of us are just ready to get going with it because we know it is inevitable. The waiting is making everyone restless.

CHAPTER TEN
PUSHING THROUGH THE GUSTAV LINE

19 May 1944

I've never seen anything like the last few days. There was no moon the night the assault started. It was a dark night and we let loose with the greatest artillery barrage I've ever heard. That was 8 days ago. It seems like longer ago than that. For 30 minutes, as I lay on the ground with the infantry, waiting for our move, our artillery fired a tremendous barrage before our attack. Twelve artillery battalions firing everything from 75 mm howitzers, 105s, all the way up to the 155mm Long Toms and the big 240 mm howitzers. Thousands of shells. The surrounding countryside was lit up with the flash of what had to be one of the biggest artillery barrages ever.

Lying on the ground in the dark, tense & scared waiting for our time to jump off, lots of things run through your mind – even with the deafening noise of the artillery barrage. We knew that ahead of us were mines, machine guns, mountainous terrain, heavy guns, fortifications and an experienced enemy who had been preparing for this moment. And they were every bit as tough as we had heard. But we had been preparing too. As we moved out over open ground that night, following the rolling barrage, I couldn't imagine what the next week would be like. I don't think anyone could.

The first couple of days were terrible. The most scared I've ever been. I was attached with K Company. We lost a lot of men

61

trying to take a couple of hills. There were enemy pillboxes everywhere it seemed. Every gain we made was met with a counter attack. German fire took its toll as we tried to move forward. Men were being cut down all around me. At full strength, K Company was about 185 men. When we finally reached Hill 69 at dawn, there were 39 of us left: 35 enlisted men and 4 officers. Lots of good men lost. Boys I had trained with. Boys I had been with since Camp Shelby. Gone forever. Their bodies lifeless, lying on the ground, maimed & bloody. There were times there that I wasn't sure any of us would make it. It was the worst thing I had ever seen.

With so few of us left once we took the hill, it was useless for K to continue to attack, so what was left of K Company was put into defensive positions with soldiers of I Company on Hill 69.

I was immediately reassigned to E Company as FO as they continued their movement. Our bombers and artillery were working over the hilltop town of Castellonorato in preparation for our assault. The German artillery in Castellonorato had been pounding our troops, so we had to take the town before we could move anywhere else. By the night of May 15, we had taken Castellonorato.

The next day, as E Company moved out of Castellonorato we were crossing this big rolling field toward Mt. Campesi, another stronghold for enemy artillery. About halfway across, the German's let loose on us with everything they had. They were firing from Mt. Campesi & Trivio. They had us pinned down in that field for over 30 hours, getting hit hard by German artillery, mortars, & automatic weapons. It was another bad situation, but we were able to get out of it because we pulled together. We were finally able to locate their firing positions and take them out, allowing us to move.

We looked out for each other. That's the way it is in battle. With the noise, blood, smoke, and confusion, sometimes all you can do is try to help the man next to you and take the next step. You just do because it has to be done. We did what had to be done, but nothing can prepare you for what we've experienced during the last week.

I've seen more death now than I could ever imagine. I've seen people blown up & maimed. I've killed people. Not just with artillery fire, but with my carbine. That is hard to get out of my mind. Boys dying holding their guts in their hands while you are trying to help them, even though you really can't do much for them. Things I will never forget.

It doesn't make sense, but you have to keep going. You have to take care of the boys around you. Try to keep them alive. And they do the same for you.

Right now, I'm tired. I thank God I am still alive.

Information excerpted from the commendation of the Silver Star Medal awarded to Lt. B.B. Darnell for actions in May, 1944, written by Capt. George J. Brehm, 328th F.A.:

"Gallantry in action as a forward observer with a front line Infantry Company. The company being in close contact with the enemy, was pinned down by small arms & automatic fire. Lt. Darnell left his observation post, a place of safety, and worked his way forward to a position from which he observed and adjusted artillery fire. Knocking out enemy resistance and allowing the front line company to advance and capture the assigned objective."

(Continued next page).

Silver Star Commendation by Capt. Brehm on behalf of Lt. Darnell (continued):

"Mountainous terrain. The enemy was located 1500 yards northwest of Castellonorato, Italy. The command had suffered approximately 15% casualties during this action. He knocked out two machine gun nests, killing numerous enemy personnel (40) thereby allowing company to advance and capture assigned objective without suffering further casualties

During the period of 16th & 17th of May, 1944, 2nd Lt. B.B. Darnell was attached to 2nd Battalion, 337th Infantry, as an Artillery forward observer. He moved with "E" Company, one of the assault companies, during the entire period.

The Infantry Company had taken Castellonorato and had started to advance in a northwesterly direction toward Mt. Campesi. They had to cross 1500 yards of low, flat terrain between two commanding hills, Castellonorato and Mt. Campesi. They had traversed approximately eight or nine hundred yards of this distance when the enemy opened up with continuous heavy automatic small arms, mortar, and artillery fire, holding up the advance of this unit for approximately thirty-six hours.

During this period, Lt. Darnell remained in close contact with the forward elements, giving supporting fires on close-in targets."

(Continued next page).

Silver Star Commendation by Capt. Brehm on behalf of Lt. Darnell (continued):

"I had an observation post on the forward nose of Castellonorato, overlooking the entire situation. Lt. Darnell could have withdrawn to my position of comparative safety, but he knew that he was covered by fire from this observation post on targets he could not see, so he chose to remain with the forward elements in order to continue his close-in fire support. His fire missions were conducted on targets close in front of the infantry in wooded terrain and gullies that were defilade to use on Castellonorato. All of these missions were conducted under the most adverse conditions as the enemy fire was continuous and heavy

Some of the fire conducted by Lt. Darnell enabled the 3rd Battalion, 337th Infantry, on our left to move forward and tie in with us to make a joint push forward. This push was successful and we rolled forward and took Mt. Campesi and four thousand yards of terrain beyond, as well as the towns of Trivio and Marinola by noon on the 18th of May, 1944.

Lt. Darnell could have withdrawn to my observation post and performed his duty satisfactorily. But his actions in voluntarily remaining far forward, and carrying out his missions with complete disregard of personal safety, show ample evidence of personal heroism far beyond the normal call of duty."

This August 2014 photo is taken from the forward edge of Castellonorato where Capt. Brehm's observation post may have been when he was observing the battle in the valley below prior to recommending Lt. Darnell for a Silver Star. Mt. Campesi is the closest hill on the left, Trivio & Marinola are on the mountain on the right.

The view in this 2014 photo above is from Mt Campesi, looking across the valley toward Castellonorato (the town on the hill on the upper left) where Capt. Brehm's observation post was located.

23 May 1944

We have pushed through the Gustav Line and the Germans are now on the run. Even in their retreat, though, they are skilled in delaying tactics that keep us from catching them. Right now we are a part of a pursuing force with the 337th Infantry and yesterday moved from Formia toward Itri where the Germans engaged us. When we captured Itri, it was the most devastated small town I had seen. Rubble everywhere. It was hard to find even two bricks still together. The combination of Allied bombing and our artillery had demolished every building in the town it seemed. The Germans had left in a hurry, even leaving a couple of their big 170mm guns that they had been pounding us with. That is two less guns they have to fire on us.

It is easy to begin to hate the Germans. You hate them because they've killed your buddies, they're trying to kill you, they're keeping you from being home, and they caused this whole mess of suffering. I don't know if I've ever hated anyone, but hating them makes what we have to do here easier.

I'm was with the 1st Battalion of the 337th. We got within 1 mile of Terracina before being forced to withdraw to Mt. Croce.

The Germans infiltrated our positons on Mt. Croce. 1st Battalion bore the brunt of the attack and fought for 36 hours without rest. 2nd Battalion relieved us for the assault on Terracina.

Tonight we are about 3000 yards south of Mt Croce. Batteries are firing on Nazi positions around Terracina. The Germans have fortified their positions in the town because of its importance in protecting Rome. Also, we have to go through Terracina, if we are to bust out our troops trapped on the beachhead at Anzio. If we can link up with them, then we can push on to Rome.

Men of the 339th Infantry of the 85th Division near Formia, Italy, in May, 1944.
National Archives photo.

Infantry approaching Itri in May, 1944. *National Archives photo.*

27 May 1944

Terracina fell on the 24th and the troops at Anzio smashed out the next day. After 49 days of operations, today we were relieved from front-line combat and have moved to a rest area near Sabaudia. Sabaudia is a town Mussolini built on the coast in 1935, so it is all new. There has been little fighting here, so everything is in pretty good shape. The men are happy to be here. Green grass & shade trees! And the sea is beautiful. We have good weather.

The food here is good too. We've got fresh eggs from somewhere – a whole lot better than the powdered ones. While we are in combat, we have to eat what we can carry – usually C or K rations or a D bar (a chocolate bar with vitamins in it). The food here is a welcome break from that.

We are all exhausted, having come through situations we could have never imagined. Everyone is so tired. Sleep doesn't come easy some nights. Sometimes it's a sleep filled with thoughts of those you killed, you've seen killed, and those buddies who will never go home.

I wrote Mildred tonight. With the Army censors, it is hard to tell the folks back home much, so most of us just write that we are fine and things are going good. No need to get them worried anyway. I wish I could talk with her about things. I mean really talk to her about the things I've seen and done – the good and the bad. She is so easy to talk to. She understands and cares for me.

I hope we get to stay here a while. Even with what we've been through, there is a positive feeling among the men now. With our victories, we all hope this will be over soon and we can head home.

28 May 1944

Went to church today. It was really good to sit in a peaceful place without anything exploding above or around you. The chaplains here do a good job. It is good to be able to talk with them sometimes. One reason I write in this journal is because it helps me to work through some of the things that happen and sometimes express thoughts I can't say to the other boys here. We don't talk about it much, but all this killing affects you. Makes you numb.

Around our kitchen at meal times, civilian children would gather with pails and pots to get any food we would throw away. It is hard to eat with those big brown eyes watching every bite you take, hoping for some. It goes right to your heart. Lots of the boys just dumped their mess kit into the children's pails, as we didn't have the heart to eat in front of them.

CHAPTER ELEVEN
ON THROUGH ROME

29 May 1944

Well we got one full day and two nights at Sabaudia. I think the higher ups are concerned with losing our momentum and want to push hard for Rome now. The men are exhausted, but everybody is ready to take Rome. We loaded into trucks & jeeps earlier today and headed out of the rest area. As we left, lots of Italian civilians of all ages lined the road, cheering, waving, and giving us the "V" for victory sign. It was an uplifting moment for all of us as we headed toward the front near Cori.

31 May 1944

23 miles south of Rome near Lariano now as the assault on Rome began this afternoon. Our artillery is firing heavily into the wooded, hilly terrain at German positions as we advance toward them. I'm moving with the infantry. Enemy planes have been bombing us – even our batteries have been bombed and strafed by the planes. No casualties in the batteries so far though. Right now, there is no place safe from enemy fire. Our air corps fighters are active and that helps keep the German planes away from us.

2 June 1944

The 337th has been smashing away at the German resistance in this area. This morning as we advanced across a field towards a location where German artillery that fired on us yesterday had been set up, an older Italian man ran up to us and kept saying "Tedeschi" which means German in Italian. We thought he was telling us that there were Germans waiting to ambush us. We finally figured out he was asking if we were Germans. When he realized we were Americans he threw his arms around one of the men and handed him a bunch of flowers. He was very happy that we were making the Germans leave his area.

Continue to call in fire missions and all told, the Battalion has fired over 40 missions today, pounding away in support of the 337th. We continue to get bombed by enemy planes, but no casualties from that. Seem to have Jerry on the run. Tonight we have moved to Mt. Castelaccio. Right now, the 85th is two miles ahead of the rest of the 5th Army and moving fast toward Rome. Looks like the Custer Division could be the first Allied troops in Rome.

3 June 1944

Our orders changed today as we moved into a position ½ mile south of Rocca Priora. The brass changed the direction of the 85th's advance, turning sharply northwest and cutting across Highway 7, effectively cutting off enemy forces retreating up the highway toward Rome.

4 June 1944

With the retreating Germans cut off, the main body of the 85th headed back toward Rome, but by that time other units of the 5th Army had beat us and had already entered the outskirts of the city.   Tonight, we are 5 miles southwest of Rome at Roma Vecchia.   The Germans have left Rome and headed north.   Still have to worry about a few stragglers and pockets of resistance, but tomorrow, we should enter Rome!   Rome is the first capital of an Axis country to fall to the Allies – hopefully this means the end of the war is near.

We have taken lots of German prisoners today.   Some of their officers are arrogant. They seem to think they are better than us. But a lot of the enlisted men just look scared and tired.   We send them back behind the lines, then some other soldiers take them further back where I suppose they are processed and interrogated.

The Germans are abandoning their positions rapidly.   Among the things we found were German gas masks.   They don't leave those unless they are really retreating in a hurry.   We also found some of their food, including a dozen cans of King Oscar sardines.   Those sardines were good.   Unless the food we find is canned, we don't touch it because it could be poisoned.   Have to watch for booby-traps on the things they leave behind too.

5 June 1944

We left our position early this morning and moved through Rome.   It was an unbelievable sight.   We went right by the ancient Colosseum.   It is hard to believe that it has been there almost 1500 years, through all those wars, all that history, good and bad, going on around it.   They say that in all of Roman history, we are the only army to ever conquer Rome from the south.   Even the great Hannibal couldn't do it.   Before this, it was thought impossible because of the rugged mountain terrain. That's understandable - it seemed impossible to us at times.

It was hard to believe that the destruction of war had bypassed the city with only a few shell holes and craters on the outskirts.

While there were still a few snipers left behind, the Germans left Rome without further damage and headed further north into the mountains. They supposedly have been digging in and building fortifications in those mountains for the last year – their last line of defense in Italy.

As we entered Rome, I was in a truck, with other troops in jeeps or on foot. There were lots of civilians in the street celebrating the liberation of their city. They didn't seem worried at all about snipers. They waved and cheered as we passed. Most of our boys were more impressed with the beautiful signorinas than anything else they saw in Rome! A few of the women would hug the boys and even give them wine. None of us had ever seen anything like this.

The liberation of Rome is also the one of our first tangible signs that the enemy may be weakening. They are fleeing our advance, even if they are fighting hard every step backwards. Gives us all hope we can end this soon.

We didn't stop in Rome. We continued north, pursuing the Germans who had already prepared defensive positions to fall back.

As we left Rome, we headed up highway 2 and tonight we are in position about 8 miles north of the city. What a day!

American troops passing by the Colosseum in Rome in June 1944.
National Archives photo.

An American column snakes through Rome's Piazza Del Popolo before pressing north in pursuit of the retreating German armies. National Archives photo.

7 June 1944

We got word today that Allied forces have crossed the English Channel and landed at Normandy in a major assault to establish a western front in France. The biggest amphibious landing in history. This is big news and has to help us. It will be hard for the Germans to fight us here, the troops landing in Normandy, and the Russians coming from the east all at the same time. We remain in position just north of Rome tonight. Our prayers are with those boys in Normandy. We know what they are headed into.

After going through some of the things we've been through, we've become conditioned to discussing the dead and wounded. Men who have been through some of the worst things imaginable are able to smile and laugh shortly thereafter. Even the locals show little emotion as they search through the rubble of their town. The impact of some of the things we've seen, seems to come later, when you have time to think about it, when you are alone.

8 June 1944

We were on the move today, chasing the enemy. As we headed north on highway 2, it was obvious the Germans were in a mess. Our planes had caught them in the open country north of Rome as they fled. Bombed out, burned out, and abandoned trucks, tanks, motorcycles, & equipment were strewn along both sides of the road. So were dead German soldiers. It was not a pretty sight. They are fleeing so fast, that don't even try to take their dead with them now. Some Italians are scavenging what they can from the bodies. We know if it was us laying there, they would be taking what they could off of our bodies too. This war isn't pretty for anybody.

As we moved north, we encountered fire from machine gun positions they had set up to delay us. Their buzzsaws are dangerous weapons that can do a lot of damage. They fire twice as fast as our machine guns and caused several casualties today.

The Germans are retreating, but they are doing everything they can to slow us down. In addition to the machine gun positions, they've blown up bridges, mined the roads, and left snipers in buildings.

As we approached Monterosi, we went into position just south of the town. We hadn't been there long when the town fell to our infantry, so we moved a few miles up the road, to just north of the town, where we are tonight.

10 June 1944

Still just north of Monterosi. Not firing much today. Most of the activity seems to be the taking of German prisoners who are coming in by the dozens now. They seem scattered and confused as if they were left behind by their units. It's obvious they didn't expect us to move as fast as we have.

As we were taking prisoners and disarming them today, I found a knife on one of them like I had never seen. I was told it was a paratrooper knife. It has a blade that comes out by gravity if you press a button and flick your wrist. This is supposedly for cutting ropes if their chutes get tangled or caught in something. On the other end it has what looks like a big ice pick, but apparently they use that to help undo knots in rigging. I've never seen a knife like it, so I think I will keep it.

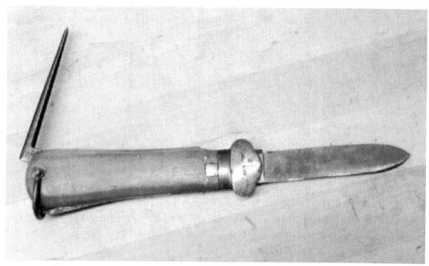

German paratrooper knife Lt. Darnell took from German soldier

Going north on Highway 2 is some beautiful country. Gently rolling land with green fields. You can look for miles across the pastures, olive groves, and vineyards.

We found a good well here so we have good water. Finding good drinking water has turned out to be more of a problem that I figured it would be here in Italy. Water in shell holes is okay if you put some purification pills in it. I know some boys who have filled their canteens from a stream and then later found out there were dead Germans up stream. We have been warned about poisoned wells, but so far I haven't heard of anyone running across one. Usually we do okay though until we can find a well or spring in a town where civilians are using the water. You just want to make sure you don't get too low, because some days it is hard to find.

11 June 1944

Yesterday, we were relieved from operations by a division of Algerian infantry that was part of the French Expeditionary Corps. I'm glad they are on our side – tough looking men.

Tonight we are at Castel Porziano, a rest & training area southwest of Rome. Apparently this place was built for the King of Italy – it is something else. A lot different from where we've been. Everyone is glad to be out of the front for a while. The Custer Division has been in combat 60 out of the last 62 days. Just yesterday, we were 42 miles past Rome, pursuing the Germans. It is good to be out of the line tonight. Who knows how long we will be here, but I'm glad we're here.

In training we were told that a soldier could not handle the continued stress of living at the front lines under constant shelling and danger for more than 30 days without losing some of his fighting abilities. We have been in combat twice that long, so it is good to be here now.

I have seen a couple of boys who have been evacuated for battle fatigue. It's not a pretty sight. One of them went berserk after hearing the first shell go over. Running around screaming. Another just shook and kept saying he was as good as dead. Neither one of them needed to be in the line. They were a danger to themselves and those of us around them.

12 June 1944

It is really good to be out of the front line for a few days. This place is pretty nice. Of course we don't just lay around. We have a pretty strict daily schedule of calisthenics, foot-drill, classes and section training each morning, with maintenance, care and cleaning of equipment, organized games and swimming, each afternoon. We've put together a Battery C softball team, so I'm enjoying getting to play ball some.   Word is that there will be passes to Rome soon.

13 June 1944

This area has lots of fruit trees such as apple, peach, and plums. There are also some black olive trees.   We've been able to get some fresh fruit and have found a few gardens.   I've been able to trade my cigarettes with some of the Italians.   The best thing I've had is a couple fresh tomatoes today.   They are just getting ripe, but they are really good.   We've seen several grape vines, but the grapes aren't ripe yet.   Since I don't smoke, I've got plenty of cigarettes to trade for things.   They are better than money around here.

Got 3 letters yesterday – one from Geraldine, one from Flossie, and one from Mildred.   It is good to hear from folks back home. I will try to write everybody back soon.   Mildred's letters always make me feel better.   Her handwriting is really beautiful.   I enjoy reading about the little things that happen during her day. Makes me feel closer to her.

15 June 1944

This has been the best opportunity we've had to get our clothing in good condition since coming to Italy.   Duffle bags were returned to us, and it is easy to get some of the local women to do laundry service.   However, the quartermaster Bath and Clothing Exchange Unit was made available to us on several occasions, and I just took care of my own, using its facilities.   It is good to get things clean and in order.

Two-day passes into Rome have started for both officers and enlisted men.   Hopefully, some of us will get to visit soon.

In spite of the relaxation from front line conditions, discipline and morale remain high.

From what we have heard, it's been a tough week for the boys in France. A lot of casualties. But is sounds like we've got a good foothold there now and are pushing the Germans back. That's good news for all of us.

16 June 1944

One of the duties of officers when we aren't on the front is to read the enlisted men's mail to home and black anything that might help the enemy. I really don't see much in their mail that would. Seems a lot like prying into their private lives to me. The men know we have to do it, but I really don't like it. It is actually pretty boring. We get to know a lot about our boys by doing this – sometimes too much. Most write their wife or girlfriend, but every now and then you find a guy writing both!

18 June 1944

It's Sunday and I went to church this morning. It's nice to have time to have a real service. The chaplain that preached today got to going in sort of a holy roller – tent revival style. Some of the boys from the North had never heard preaching like that! He did a good job though. He itemized his prayers, covering most everything we all pray for and ended with "Lord, please let our artillery be of good aim and do make it easier on the infantry." That got a big amen from everybody!

19 June 1944

Just got back from seeing Col. Burton who gave me my silver First Lieutenant bar. I knew I had been put up for promotion a while back, but had almost forgotten about it. I am glad to get the promotion. It will be a few more dollars to send home.

I also heard today that a number of U.S. and British troops in Italy will be moving to France to join the fight on that front. Seems like they are putting more emphasis on the Western Europe push than here in Italy. Not sure what that is going to mean for us.

I wrote a few letters tonight. Sent one to Lucille and one to Mildred. I think Lucille is more interested in me than I am in her. That started in school at Auburn and she still seems that way. We dated some, but that is all in the past for me. I don't want to hurt her feelings and I appreciate her writing, but I keep my letter to her pretty bland. It didn't take long over here with what we've been through for me to realize that Mildred is the woman I love. I knew it before I left, but with the life and death situations I've seen here, it is clearer than ever how much I love her. I start every letter I write to her with "Dearest Mildred" and sign them all "Love Always". I hope she knows that I mean it when I use those phrases. They aren't just words. She is so important to me.

Excerpts from recommendation of promotion of Second Lieutenant B.B. Darnell to the rank of First Lieutenant, from Col. Emmitt Burton, Commanding Officer of 328th Field Artillery:

"Second Lieutenant Darnell has demonstrated his leadership ability in combat under shell fire while serving as Forward Observer and Battery Executive."

"On April 20 1944 Lt. Darnell took his forward observer party to a battery observation post on a forward crest and although shelled by the enemy almost every day and every night, remained there, continually directing artillery fire on enemy installations, until relieved the night of April 26. He again took over the observation post with his party on April 30th and remained there until relieved on May 2nd. On returning to the battery after relief from the observation post he acted capably as executive of the firing battery"

"On the night of 2-3 May 1944 Lt. Darnell accompanied the control party of the supporting infantry in a "Kill or Capture" raid which resulted in the capture of two prisoners. During this time, Lt. Darnell smoked enemy observation and brought artillery fire to bear on the enemy enabling the supporting infantry to accomplish their mission. All members of the party returned safely although shelled by the enemy on their return"

21 June 1944

Even though we aren't on the front lines, it is still dangerous when you are around people with loaded guns. Last night, one of the cooks was cleaning his pistol and barely missed shooting another GI by accident. He had removed the magazine, but forgot there was a round in the chamber. Sometime during the cleaning the weapon went off. Luckily it missed the guy who was near him.

I've heard of some guys getting shot by someone who was trying out a captured German Burp Gun. The Germans use those guns with effectiveness against us. We hate them, but it is hard for our boys to not want to try one out when they find one. The bad thing is, they don't have a safety. When the bolt is pulled back and the handle is in the slot, if the gun is dropped, it will fire. I have heard of some GIs getting shot fooling around with these.

There are loaded weapons everywhere, which is one reason we are always having weapons training – just to keep everybody sharp and thinking.

27 June 1944

Just got back from two days in Rome. Quite an experience. While there we took some tours of the city that were set up by the Red Cross. We saw all of the tourist sites such as the Colosseum, the Roman Forum, St. Peters, and the Catacombs of San Sebastian. When I think of all the history in this place it is hard to believe I am here.

We headquartered out of the Fifth Army officers' club, which made it a lot easier to know what to do & see. What a sight! Famous statues, paintings and marble everywhere. Pretty amazing sights for an Alabama farm boy.

We climbed a set of stairs up to the brass ball atop the Dome of St. Peters. It had to be at least 300 steps – stone steps that were worn down over the centuries. It was hot and when we reached the ball there were 3 people already in it. From the ground it looks small, but it was actually about 10' in diameter with thick brass walls. After this we were soaked in sweat, but the view over Rome and across the Tiber River was worth it.

After we came down, we followed a guide into a chamber where Pope Pius the Tenth was on display. He had been dead for 30 years and apparently it was custom to have his mummified body on display. The Catholic boys with us were handing their rosaries to priests to have the rosaries touched to the mummy's hands, blessed, and returned. I was ready to get out of there.

We did go to some Italian restaurants, but we only ate spaghetti with tomato sauce. We were warned not to eat any meat because there is very little, if any, refrigeration available in Rome right now.

The people of Rome have had a hard time. Lots a kids on the streets begging. We give them what we can, but it is a sad sight to see.

1 July 1944

Our couple of days in Rome were too short. It was an amazing place to see. Even in war, some of the people dress like they were out of a fashion page compared to the farm folks we had seen before. The girls were very pretty.

I couldn't get over the opulence of the Vatican. The display of wealth and architecture. To a farm boy this was indeed quite a place with centuries of history. It amazed me that we were walking in the footsteps of the Caesars. It was something I had never imagined.

10 July 1944

Pretty much settled into a routine here now. Same drills, training, games, etc. It's been good for everybody to get better. The passes to Rome have been popular, with some of the boys over-doing it a little too much. There have been some who got drunk and ended up being robbed. There have been a few who didn't make it back to camp on time who have had to be disciplined. Today, a jeep carrying 3 men from Headquarters Battery overturned in a sharp curve on their way back from Rome. The accident killed one of the men and injured the other two. In the middle of a war, and he got killed in a car accident. Doesn't make sense, but I guess when your time is up, your time is up.

15 July 1944

The Battalion broke camp at Castel Porziano yesterday. We moved north along the coast road in convoy to Grossetto, then turned inland to Roccostrada. It was hot and the road was dusty. We finally stopped near Roccostrada around midnight and bivouacked in an olive grove, where we are now. Seems like the drill schedule is becoming more rigorous as we prepare the men to head back into the line. We are still some distance from the front.

This is beautiful, rolling farm land through this area called Tuscany. Even with the war damages, you can still see the vineyards, olive groves, peach and apple orchards, and grain fields that the Italian farmers try to maintain in spite of the fighting. They have really good tomatoes too if you can find a garden and trade for them. Grapes are hanging on the vine, still not ripe. There are lots of flowers, tall pines, elder, and poplar trees.

This area is about the only place we've been where there aren't big mountains. Lots of hills, but not the high mountains like we went through between Naples and Rome.

17 July 1944

Two more 105s were added to our Battery today – bringing us up to 6 guns total. We've been operating with 4 ever since we've been here, so this will be a big boost.

Some of us went out looking around the area today and I saw the biggest cows I've ever seen in my life. They were sort of grayish-white with a dark nose and skin and they had horns. The cows were almost as tall as me. It looks like they use them as oxen to pull equipment, but also for meat. They were huge.

I feel sorry for the farmers here. Their farming livelihood and farms themselves have been pretty much destroyed by the war. But they keep trying and I understand that. Cows have to be milked no matter what – if your cows haven't been killed.

20 July 1944

Yesterday morning, we moved northward again, getting closer to the front. We went through some very beautiful countryside and are now bivouacked near Rosignano Marittimo which is on the coast, just south of Pisa.

The town itself had been the scene of a very difficult battle and the fields around it are pock-marked with shell holes as far as you can see.

22 July 1944

The Italians here are very poor but, like farmers everywhere, they are willing to share what they have.   Yesterday, we met a farmer while trading for some plums.   One of the boys with me could speak some Italian and we hit it off with the farmer.   He invited us to supper at his home.   My buddies and I scrounged some flour from our cook and the farmer's wife made homemade spaghetti.   The farmer killed a chicken.   They served us a fine supper – chicken and spaghetti.   They had hidden some wine and brought it out for us.   They had their daughters sing for us.   We were all homesick and the Italian mother treated us like her sons. Her own son had been taken prisoner and was in a German labor camp somewhere up north.   It was a nice change from our normal routine.   These people really seem to value family and they are glad we are here.

24 July 1944

Although still a considerable distance from the front, we can see the flashes of our big guns and hear the heavy artillery barrages from the direction of Pisa.   There is no escaping the noise of the big guns.

Our drill schedule has been tightened up as we continue the process of reconditioning the battalion to head into the line after its rest. Every day now, we have two hour hikes, in the hottest part of the day, to help accomplish this.

28 July 1944

The entire battalion moved eastward in convoy this morning. Our new position is about six miles north of Volterra. This puts us a little closer to the front, but more centrally locates us to go in any direction the Fifth Army may need us.

Tonight we are about a half a mile from the highway in a rolling valley. As we moved east, away from the coast, we traveled through some beautiful farm land. Gently rolling hills and valleys with good soil for growing. Even with the war, you can tell that this is good farming country. Lots of vineyards and olive groves, but wheat, oats, corn fields as well. The war has damaged the fields and the crops but it looks like the farmers are still trying to do their best with them and get what they can.

My unit is actually in a peach orchard while some of the others are in patches of woods that border some oat fields in the valley. The trees give us excellent concealment and make this a good area to bivouac in, plus the peaches are ripe! I actually think the boys are ready to head back to the front. We all want to get this over with and, unfortunately, that probably won't happen if we aren't headed north.

29 July 1944

Happy birthday to me! – 23 years old today. Glad to be alive to see 23.

As usual, Bedcheck Charlie flew over and dropped a few bombs on us about 2300 last night. Luckily, no one was hurt. I suppose it's just harassment, but this solitary German plane comes over night after night and drops flares and bombs.

1 Aug 1944

Although we are within the sounds of the artillery guns, we are well out of range of enemy gunfire. No night-time visit from Bedcheck Charlie last night. I think our Air Corps boys have something to do with that. We have erected semi-permanent pup-tent installations and our program of preparation to re-enter the line is continuing. In addition to the drills & training, we have softball every day. The Army has made me a pretty good softball player. Back in the States, I started pitching and I do okay with it. Headquarters Battery takes softball serious and one of their better pitchers, has helped me with my pitching – even though I'm in Battery C. I guess they figure we aren't much competition for them.

8 Aug 1944

The Battalion got a new radio that we can run on batteries that allows us to get war news. We can pick up German radio and the British Broadcasting Corporation. Sounds like from the news, that victory is closer every day. There is great interest among all the men in the news and rumors start easily.

Morale is high here. While we continue to train & drill, everybody is more rested. The Battalion okayed the use of Battery Funds to purchase a beer ration for all personnel. Like always, I give mine to some of the boys and sell some. I'm a popular guy here when we get beer & cigarettes, since everybody in the Battery knows I don't use either one. I usually find a way to get some use out of them, either trading or selling.

CHAPTER TWELVE
ACROSS THE ARNO TO THE GOTHIC LINE

18 Aug 1944

On the night of the 15th, we left our bivouac area northeast of Volterra at 2330. We convoyed in trucks to an assembly area, where we arrived at 0400 in the morning.

While most of the Battalion stayed at the assembly area, some of us continued on in a forward party to our new position to dig in installations. The Battalion as a whole moved up here last night.

Right now we are in position just southwest of San Miniato, in a broad, deep valley. There are lots of grape vineyard and fruit orchards in this river valley. Our mission here is to defend the Arno River along the front of the 337ᵗʰ Infantry. We have attached to us a major (white), and three other officers (colored), together with several colored non-commissioned officers, from the 92nd (Negro) Division. This will be their first time to go into the line. When I see those boys, I can't help but think of the Wynn boys back home. I know Ninny joined the Army before I left, but I'm not sure about the others. I don't know where they are now, but I hope they're safe.

In addition to the Battalion's own eighteen 105 MM howitzers, and two 3 inch Guns, we have attached to us one Platoon of tank Destroyers, and one Battery of British heavy anti-aircraft guns, converted for ground attack. A Battery of Newfoundland 18-pound Field Artillery, also has positions in our area.

This new assignment will give us the first real opportunity to put the new six-gun battery to test since its authorization. Should allow us to rain down massive amounts of fire quickly. From what we've heard about the German fortifications ahead, we will need it.

20 Aug 1944

Tonight I'm on high ground overlooking the Arno River with my forward observation party. The Arno is a pretty big river that we are going to have to cross at some point. We are in a good observation position, but we are exposed to German artillery fire. So far, no damage.

21 Aug 1944

Still in the OP overlooking the Arno. About 2330 last night we stopped a teenage Italian boy who was making his way to our position. Said he had some information about German positions across the river. I had one of the men take him down to Battalion HQ for them to deal with. You have to be careful, there are still fascist Italians working with the Germans. The kid could be trying to get us in a trap.

We are dug in tight here. We've gotten frequent shelling most of the day, but everyone is okay. We have been able to locate some positions and called it in, returning the favor to the Germans.

25 Aug 1944

Last night we were relieved of our position at the OP overlooking the Arno and the whole battalion was moved back to a rest area a few miles behind the lines and out of artillery range for the Germans. Good to have a break, even though the Jerry planes still visit us.

29 Aug 1944

Another middle of the night move last night. This morning about 0500 we arrived in our new position near Monelupo in the Arno Valley. We have our guns set up in the valley, but none of our positions can be reached without coming under enemy observation from Mount Albano. Seems like they are always on the higher ground looking down on us. Luckily there are lots of trees here, so that helps hide some of our activity, but we know they can see us.

1 Sept 1944

About 0200 this morning, we moved into rendezvous in our old firing position near San Miniato. We held here as preparations were being made for the Arno River crossing. Everybody has been working furiously preparing for the crossing. Our job is to support the attack of the 1st Armored Division across the Arno. Crossing the river leaves everybody exposed to fire, so our artillery support is important in keeping the enemy from letting loose on the boys crossing. We expect lots of resistance.

Capt. Dempsey had quite an unusual experience late this afternoon. He was sitting in his tent when a German officer walked in, surprising him. The unarmed German was agitated and cursing saying there were "no gentlemen in the American Army". Seems the German was upset because he had been trying to surrender, and every soldier he ran into told him they were too busy, just keep moving to the rear – which brought him to our position.

Capt. Dempsey questioned him about what was on the other side of the Arno, the German told him "nothing – they have all pulled back." Plans are to send an infantry squad across the river later tonight to see if he is telling the truth.

2 Sept 1944

Capt. Dempsey's visitor yesterday was right – the Germans have all pulled back and the crossing of the river was uneventful. This morning we were moving north with the 1st Armored toward the Arno. We were told to move as close to the Arno as possible and hold. When we got there, we found out that patrols had found very few Germans on the other side, so most of the Division we were attached to had already crossed the river. But our orders were not to cross because we were going to revert to control of the 85th again. Then it began to rain and rain hard. We've been waiting here most of the afternoon, in the rain, awaiting orders to return to our Division.

If it keeps raining like this, we will be stranded and can't move in any direction.

3 Sept 1944

Still by the Arno. We're dug in, waiting for orders. Even though the rain finally stopped this afternoon, nothing is dry. We're in a defensive position and everything is soaked. Looks like another muddy night in a hole.

Today is Mildred's birthday. I wanted to write her a letter to let her know I'm thinking about her, but everything here is a mess with the rain. It will have to wait.

4 Sept 1944

We finally received the order to return to the 85th, but that was easier said than done. This morning we headed back the same way we came 3 days ago. Bridges were washed out and we had to ford creeks. The mud in Italy is something else. It got so deep that even on the roads, it went over the wheels on the trucks.

When you walk in it, it just clings to your shoes. The weight of the mud on your shoes builds up and makes walking tough. These roughout shoes we have just aren't made for Italian mud – they don't shed water and take too long to dry. I've heard that there is a new combat boot being issued, but it hasn't made its way to us yet.

It wasn't an easy trip, but we finally made it back and are in rendezvous now near Malmantile with the rest of the 85th. Everything I have is wet and muddy and we didn't fire one round on this excursion. What next?

6 Sept 1944

Yesterday we received orders to occupy positions on the north side of the Arno, so last night we moved back up north. We forded the river in pitch black, west of Florence, without incident. Today we are set up in position on the outskirts of Florence. Been relatively slow, only firing a few harassing missions.

Tonight, we are north of the Arno (finally) and safe.

8 Sept 1944

There are farms in this valley and the countryside is beginning to take on the brownish colors of late summer and early fall. Its harvest time, but with shortages of everything, it has to be difficult for them. I traded some cigarettes to a local farmer for some onions he had hanging up to dry. We discovered a long time ago that if you have an onion or a pepper, you can add some flavor to your field rations. They will come in handy.

10 Sept 1944

This morning we moved through Florence.   Like most of the places we've been there is evidence of demolition and destruction, but most seems to be on the outskirts.   We had a glimpse of some of the famous buildings as we passed through the city center on our way north.

As we headed up Highway 65, we knew what we were headed toward.   Ahead of us is the Germans' last line of defense in Italy, the Gothic Line.   A battle area of their choosing that they have been fortifying for almost two years.   Supposedly, their engineers have worked on their positions here longer than they did the Gustav line in the south. These mountain ranges in Italy just seem to get bigger and bigger.   From the information we have, we know just a few miles ahead of us will be the toughest battles yet.   We also know that if we can breach this line, Germany's underside would be exposed and the war could end quickly.

Tonight, we are on the north side of the Sieve River and are in position near Bosso.   The men are tense knowing what is ahead. It's Sunday and after everybody got dug in, the chaplain had a prayer service that was well attended.

The Ponte Vecchio was the only bridge left standing by the retreating Germans in Florence. Photo from National Archives.

11 Sept 1944

This morning we saw the massive mountain heights of the Gothic Line. It overlooks the entire Sieve valley where we are. Even from here we can spot emplacements and bunkers high in the mountains overlooking our positions. They have constructed their defenses to funnel us into their fire zones. Luckily, in our position right now, we are protected from their direct fire by a low hill. Although once we move, we won't have that protection.

These mountains are covered with a few chestnut trees, some scrub oak, and some pines where there is enough soil to support them. Many of the mountains are just bare rocky slopes with razorback ridges and sheer cliffs. Rough going ahead for us.

There aren't many roads through the mountains either. The 1-1/2 ton trucks won't pull the guns up these mountains. The GMC 2-1/2 ton trucks do better, but roads are bad. Mules and mule-skinners are as important as any general right now. I think the Army has bought every mule in Italy to help move supplies in these hills.

The Allies used mule trains with Italian mule-skinners to move ammo and food up to the troops in the mountains.

Photo from the U.S. Army Series on the History of WW2.

CHAPTER THIRTEEN
DEATH THROUGHOUT THESE MOUNTAINS

12 Sept 1944

We got our orders earlier today. Tomorrow we are moving forward, right into the teeth of the Gothic Line. My FO party is assigned to move with Company I, 3rd Battalion, 337th Infantry in the attack on Mt. Pratone. I've been with the various units of the 337th a lot over the last several months. We do a good job working together – good boys, so I'm glad I'm going to be with them. I expect the next few days will be intense, but we are ready to go.

15 Sept 1944

We jumped off a couple of days ago and were pinned down for two days trying to make it up Mt. Pratone. It was the most intense fire from the enemy I have come across. We were able to call in enough fire for us to finally be able to continue the attack. We are making advances, but it is slow and difficult. The enemy is well placed in the mountains and we are totally exposed trying to make our way up against their fire. Lots of casualties.

17 Sept 1944

These mountains are unlike any we've been through yet. Not only are they high and difficult to climb but they are jagged with cliffs, gorges, and ravines that make every step dangerous. Will we ever be in flat land again? No sleep for anyone as we push ahead. The boys have hardly had a chance to eat. This is the worst terrain we've been through. If we find a goat path to follow, the Germans have their guns set up to fire on the trail. They prepared their defenses well and we are paying the price.

A boy had his arm blown completely off near me today. We were hugging the ground as we were getting shelled. One hit near us and I hear the boy screaming and see his left arm is gone... just completely gone almost up to his shoulder. I crawled over to him. Blood was spurting from where his arm use to be. Shells were continuing to land near us, and he was still screaming. I put my belt up as high as I could on what was left of his arm to try to slow the bleeding. I stayed with him and tried to calm him down. He was going into shock. Finally, a medic was able to get over to help him. I don't know if he made or not. He lost a lot of blood - a lot of it is still all over me.

19 Sept 1944

There is death all through these mountains. Lots of casualties. Every step seems to be under fire. No choice but to keep going and keep killing or be killed. You get to the point that all you want to do is kill the enemy. You know you have to in order to get where you have to go. I've seen boys go berserk with all the killing. No one can blame them. That's what we're here for – to kill the Germans. You have to get good at it to survive. I pray I don't lose my life in all this, but I also pray I don't lose my humanity. That would be worse.

Tonight I'm with K Company. I Company moved back to reserve, but there are no more forward observers in the Battalion, so I'm moving with K now. Tomorrow we begin the assault on the right flank Mt. La Fine. Dug in my hole and it is starting to rain – cold rain.

Information from the recommendation for the award of an Oak Leaf Cluster to Silver Star filed by Capt. William J. Dempsey, Jr, 328th F.A., on behalf of Lt. B.B. Darnell for his actions from September 13 – October 4, 1944:

"On 13 September 1944 Lt. Darnell led an artillery observer party moving with Company I, 3rd Battalion, 337th Infantry Regiment in the attack on Mt. Pratone. This enemy stronghold was 1081 meters high and covered with an intricate network of enemy defenses. In the first day of the attack up the precipitous slopes of this mountainous objective the most intense enemy artillery, mortar, and small arms fire was encountered, rendering further advance impossible and pinning down the company. This situation continued throughout the next day. Working his way forward in spite of this intense enemy fire, Lt. Darnell placed himself in a position to observe enemy locations on Mt. Pratone and acting directly in conjunction with the Regimental Commander, adjusted the artillery of the 85th Division, II Corps and V Army until he had Mt. Pratone covered with one of the most terrific barrages of the entire campaign. It enabled the infantry to continue the attack successfully and Mt. Pratone was taken that night.

Following this, Lt. Darnell moved with I Company cutting the road from Firenzuola to Castel del Rio. In this move more than 200 Germans were caught moving along the road. Lt. Darnell blocked their escape routes by placing artillery fire in front of them and in back of them, and then upon them until they were completely disorganized and suffered many casualties."
(Continued on next page)

Oak Leaf Cluster for Silver Star commendation written by Capt. Dempsey on behalf of Lt. Darnell (continued):

"Following this action, I Company was placed in reserve and K Company continued in the assault. Since there were no other observers with the 3rd battalion, Lt. Darnell went forward in the attack with K Company against the right flank of Mt. La Fine. This attack took place in a pouring rain storm and biting cold over extremely rugged and mountainous terrain heavily defended by the enemy with small arms, mortar, and machine guns as well as artillery fire. In spite of these difficulties and extreme fatigue, Lt. Darnell covered the objective with such intense and accurate artillery fire that the infantry was able to continue is advance and capture its objective. Here for two days, exposed to cold, rain, and severe enemy fire, he shot in defensive fires and brought them down with devastating effect on the enemy counter-attacks. In the course of this fighting he ran a heavy fever and caught cold but refused to be evacuated.

On the right of Mt. La Fine, the 349th Infantry of the 88th Division were being held up by five German artillery pieces which were pounding them continually as they tried to advance. Lt. Darnell located the German artillery and adjusted both the Division and Corps artillery, completely destroying them and enabling the 349th to advance. About two hours later, he located two German machine guns which were firing on the 349th Infantry and silenced them. By this time, Lt. Darnell's illness and fatigue had greatly increased and he was advised to be evacuated by the medical officer of the infantry. He refused to do this and moved with the infantry in the attack on Guignola, still under intense enemy fire and continuous cold and heavy rainfall." **(Continued on next page)**

Oak Leaf Cluster for Silver Star commendation written by Capt. Dempsey on behalf of Lt. Darnell (continued):

"*Here K Company was relieved and I Company again placed in a frontal assault on Hill 752. As yet without relief or rest and in great need of medical attention, Lt. Darnell switched his forward party from K Company to I Company and went into the face of withering enemy small arms, machine gun, and mortar fire. For two days and nights they attacked frontally and were pinned down in a mass of rock, mud, and water. Finally Lt. Darnell brought artillery fire down on the ridge to the right of Hill 752 and the infantry successfully advanced and captured it, outflanking their objective. When Lt. Darnell was relieved and returned to the battery he was staggering from sheer fatigue and illness. He had been in the assault with the infantry for twenty-one days. Two different forward observer parties had been with him and were completely exhausted. He had always been with the spearhead of the attack, never faltering, never asking for relief and even refusing it when he was told to take it. Upon return to his organization he was placed under immediate medical care, but refused evacuation to a hospital, remaining with his battery which was moving in the attack in support of the infantry. Lt. Darnell's devotion to duty, his extreme courage in the face of withering enemy fire, severe illness and extreme fatigue as well as his superior leadership at the most critical moments were an inspiration to his men and are in the finest tradition of the service.*"

7 Oct 1944

The last three weeks have been the hardest of my life. It has seemed like a lifetime of mud, cold rain, strain, fear, noise, blood, and prayers. Right now, I'm back with C Battery but I've been out with infantry since we started the assault. So much has happened, I can't even write it down. The most difficult fighting I've seen. The most death I've seen. The most dead bodies I've seen. War is worse than most people think or they read in the newspapers back home. The scary part is that you become numb to it. You have to in order to keep going.

The Germans had every possible angle planned everywhere we moved. On most of the hills, our artillery fire couldn't outflank them. The only choice was frontal assault, just like they wanted. Their positions were well prepared. Pillboxes dug in with such thick concrete, fortified so well that our artillery couldn't knock them out. Mortar fire and automatic weapons fire from concrete emplacements on top of every hill. Our boys were scorched over & over again. There were terrible losses.

It's been raining for days. Mud is everywhere. It's cold in these mountains. I'm tired and I've got a fever, cold or something. My body aches, but I've got to keep going – just like everyone else.

Since I got back with the battery yesterday, we've had to move the guns so that we can support the infantry better, but positions are scarce here. We moved over a treacherous, slippery, ridge trail and right now are just off the top of a ridge at Spedaletto. I've got to get some sleep. I'm tired and need sleep.

8 Oct 1944

Since the Normandy landing, we've been short of infantry here in Italy. They've moved lots of troops to France. We don't have enough of anything here now. Seems like the brass thinks France is more important than here. People are calling Italy the forgotten front. They couldn't forget it if they had seen just one of the lines of mules moving down the mountain paths with canvas wrapped bundles on their back. Bundles with muddy GI boots sticking out of them. Boys that will never go home now. I know I will never forget it.

Battle can test your faith, but if you pay attention, sometimes you can see God's hand in even the worst of it. I know God is still in control – even with the horrible things we've seen. Over the last few weeks, I've killed lots of Germans. That's the way war is. I pray a lot about it.

It was really bad when we caught a convoy of Germans on the road north of Firenzuola a couple of weeks ago. Most ended up surrendering, but before they did, I called fire down all around them that was responsible for lots of death. It was my duty, and it saved American lives, but an ambush like that bothers me. Then a few days later, we spotted another column of German's headed north further up the same road outside of Castel del Rio. They were headed north toward Bologna. It was early morning, right before daylight. I had them in a place where they had nowhere to go and it would be a complete surprise when we started shelling them. I was on the radio to the CP as the sun was coming up. I knew it was going to be a massacre. As I was waiting, I prayed – for myself, the boys with me, and for those who I would be responsible for killing. About that time, the heaviest, fastest moving fog I've ever seen descended on those mountains and that valley. I couldn't see anything down below me. There was no way we could fire with that fog – I couldn't locate anything. While I know I shouldn't say it, I was actually relieved that we had to abort the ambush. I believe it was God showing me he is still in control, no matter what. He saved some German lives that day, but he also saved a part of me.

I'm feeling better now. My fever is down, so I'm moving out with the infantry again in the morning. Monterenzio is still not in our hands and we are headed that way.

16 Oct 1944

Right now I am at the Evac Hospital near Pietramala, and lucky to be alive. The morning of Oct. 12, I was with the 337th as we assaulted Monterenzio. The enemy was determined to hold the area. Every advance was met with a counterattack. Every hill, town and group of buildings had to be desperately fought for, often at close quarters. My FO party was right in the thick of it with the other boys. I felt this sharp pain and something burning across my belly. I knew I had been hit. When the infantry medic was able to get to me, he cleaned it up and taped it back together best he could. Not sure if it was a bullet or shrapnel, but it cut the front of my abdomen without hitting any organs, so I was lucky. Guess it wasn't my time yet.

The morning of the 14th we were relieved by the 339th Infantry, and they were able to get me to this hospital. The doctors cleaned everything best they could and sewed it all up. They found some fragments of rock, dirt, and some metal. They said it cut my abdomen muscles, but didn't damage any organs. I'm sore but feeling okay. There have been lots of casualties the last couple of weeks. There are a lot of boys worse than me here.

17 Oct 1944

This hospital was just set up a few days ago and they are still working on it. It was good for me that it is here or I would have had to been taken all the way to Florence. This is a lot closer. Right now it is the northernmost Army hospital in Italy.

The doctor said there is a risk of infection to my wound. The medic did the best he could, but I was still in the line for a couple of days after getting wounded. There weren't enough medics with so many casualties – they had their hands full. The Doc said as dirty as the wound was, I will probably always have a little bit of Italy in me.

Now I am getting regular shots of penicillin. I've been getting shots every four hours – left arm, right arm, and then my rear. I am feeling like a pin cushion. Still have a few more days of that.

Lots of men here have been wounded fighting in the mountains, but there are a few that I wonder about. They seem okay to me. Some people will do about anything to get away from the front. I've heard stories of people eating soap just to get sick to get sent out of the line. I've even heard of some people shooting their foot to get out of the front. Combat is hard on everybody, but these guys that do this ought to be court-martialed and put in the stockade. Too many good boys are giving too much. I don't have much use for these ones that won't pull their weight.

19 Oct 1944

Feeling a lot better now, but I am pretty sore in my midsection. Doc said it will be sore a long time and I have to be careful not to tear it back open as the wound heals. They have offered me morphine, but I'm afraid of that stuff. I've tried to keep it to a minimum. I've seen to many boys get messed up by it.

Most of the doctors and top nurses here are from the University of Virginia. I found out they put this hospital unit together at the university. They started out in North Africa and have moved all the way up Italy as the front moved. In the last few months, a lot of medical units have moved from Italy to France, so these people have had their hands full. There are new casualties coming in every day.

20 Oct 1944

The doctor says I will be released later today. I am ready to get out of this hospital. It's been good to get some rest, but it's time to get out. There are some who need the medical attention more than me. I'm lucky that I haven't had any serious infection since the wound was full of dirt & mud by the time I got here. The penicillin is supposed to keep it from getting infected. Seems to be working because it's healing well. I just have to keep it clean and have it checked by the medics if I have any problems. A Capt. came by earlier and gave 7 of us in the ward Purple Hearts. That's a sure sign they're going to kick you back out to combat.

University of Virginia photos showing enlisted men of the 8th Evacuation Hospital setting up a ward tent (above).   Below is another UVA photo showing the unit's hospital complex in Pietramala, Italy, in late 1944.

CHAPTER FOURTEEN
BACK TO THE LINE AS WINTER SETS IN

21 Oct 1944

I caught a ride late yesterday afternoon and I'm back in position with the 328th *in a ravine near Molinetta. They call this place "Dead Ass Gulch" because there were 8 dead mules laying in the creek when the Battalion first got here. I'm back with C Battery. It doesn't look like I will be going out as a forward observer anytime soon. That should give my belly a better chance of healing up. That suits me just fine.*

Looks like the final assault on the Po Valley starts tomorrow, with the infantry moving out. Maybe, if the weather holds, we can reach Bologna before winter sets in. My battery is in position, dug in, and ready. It's going to be different being back here at the gun line instead of out in the assault with the infantry.

24 Oct 1944

As soon as the infantry moved out a couple of nights ago to start their assault, the rain started. More Italian rain. They are on their first objectives, but the heavy rains have made most trails impassable, washed out bridges and all in all made an impossible situation for everybody.

We have been firing support missions for them, but our observers are having a tough time in the mud too. We continue to receive shelling in our battery area from the Germans, but we haven't had any casualties. Baker Battery hasn't been as lucky, suffering 3 casualties last night.

It is a mess right now – hard to move anywhere. It's been a tough go. Seems this area is nothing but mountains and mud.

I heard today that during the last 6 weeks, the four U.S. Infantry Divisions here have suffered over 15,000 casualties. Based on what I've seen, I believe it.

27 Oct 1944

The rains got even worse yesterday. Bologna is still about 10 miles away, but movement forward is nearly impossible. Roads & bridges are washed out. Miles on a map here don't mean anything anyway. By the time you go up and down ridges, around streams, and cliffs, zigzagging up the sides of mountains you cover 2-3 times the distance that is shown on the map.

Trench foot has become a real problem here with some of the men. Everything stays wet and dirty. You have to try to clean your feet and put on dry socks whenever you can. Hard to find anything dry right now though.

We heard today that our infantry has orders to withdraw back here, dig in and organize defensive positions. It is beginning to sound like we won't make the Po Valley before winter. The Germans had moved in reinforcements apparently before the rain started. The bad weather is making getting supplies to us difficult. Right now, everything is coming up by mule. And the bodies are going back down by mule too.

31 Oct 1944

The last couple of days have been spent on trying to improve our positions in preparation for defense. The weather is getting colder. It has started snowing some. Mud is everywhere and everything is wet. We got word today that our Battery allotment of ammo is getting cut to 100 rounds per day. Looks like our supply situation is getting worse. We can only hope the German's are having the same problems. They continue to harass us with counter-battery fire, but no significant damage.

5 Nov 1944

We continue to just sit here as it gets colder and try to dodge the enemy shelling. Seems to come about 1530 to 1700 hours every afternoon. Yesterday they landed two near the Command Post, wounding a couple of men and nicking a couple of others, including Col. Burton.

We had a gas alert last night, so everybody scrambled to get their gas mask. Some of the boys couldn't find theirs – luckily it was a false alarm. I remember during training back in the states when they used gas on us in drills. It is bad stuff. Hope we don't run into it here.

8 Nov 1944

Fifth Army has pretty much suspended offensive operations now since it has become clear now that we won't be able to reach the Po Valley before winter sets in. The Gothic Line has been breached to some degree, but in reality it is just dented. The German back up positions are almost as difficult – really not much difference. So we are still in the mountains and the Germans are as well – lots of them. And they continue to shell and bomb us regularly.

I have a good bit of soreness in my mid-section still. The wound seems to be healing, but it's nowhere near good as new.

Flag for Battery C, 328ᵗʰ Field Artillery from WWII
Photo courtesy of Bill Dempsey.

11 Nov 1944

Don't know what the Germans are up to but they are stepping up harassing us with heavy shelling. Today they fired over 100 shells into the Battalion area. One man in Able Battery was killed. They've also started sending planes to strafe and bomb us every night. The last four nights this has been a regular occurrence. We feel like sitting ducks here – they know exactly where we are, while they are dug in their bunkers higher up.

The rain & sleet turned to heavy snow today. Our supplies are having a hard time reaching us. Morale is getting to be a problem since we are just sitting here, knowing we have no immediate goal in sight other than surviving winter. No one likes the idea of spending the winter up here.

13 Nov 1944

Yesterday we received word that the British 67th FA was relieving us from front line duty – and we were all ready for that. We had been getting more & more shelling from the Germans, so we were ready to get out of that hot spot.

It was 0300 this morning before we finally were loaded and started moving out. It was a dark night and difficult to see. One of the half-tracks slipped off the muddy road twice within a mile after leaving our position. That delayed everything and when the sun started coming up, we were still in the front-line road network, well within the range of the German planes that have been visiting us regularly. It was a tense time because none of us liked the idea of being caught in convoy by those planes. Lucky for us, they didn't show up.

Tonight we are in a bivouac area on Highway 65, about 25 miles north of Florence, near Gagliano. It's actually colder here than it was near the front (we are at a higher elevation) but the Batteries are set up around some old buildings, with as many men indoors as possible. Being out of the weather in a drier place is a definite improvement.

15 Nov 1944

Gagliano is a lot like any small Italian town. The buildings are old. It is obviously not a wealthy town. It has sustained some war damage but not as bad as many of the towns we've been through. The people here are a bit reserved, but it seems soldiers and children always get along. Curious children from the town have been making friends with the boys – walking along beside them, getting a cigarette for their daddy or chocolate for themselves. It is good to see children being children.

18 Nov 1944

It is good to be away from the front where we don't get fired on every day. While this place isn't fancy, we can get dry and clean our clothes and gear. It's cold, but there is plenty of firewood. Plus, there are passes to Florence. Morale is good. We still do calisthenics, marches and section training every day, but I'm happy to do all of that to be out of the line for a while.

The Italian people here are nice to us. As tough as they have had things, they are glad the fascists and Germans are gone from this area. Even though these folks don't have much, they are better off, it seems, out here in the country and small towns than the poor people we've seen in some of the large cities.

We've had a couple of days of clear, sunny weather, so yesterday three of us went up to see Futa Pass. It's only about ten miles north of here. Futa Pass was heavily defended by the Germans and is where they expected us to try to breakthrough their line. Instead we surprised them with our assault on the adjacent Giogo Pass in Sept.

When we got to Futa Pass there was a little cafe right on top of the mountain. It was about mid-day, so we decided to get something to eat. It was cold, and the hot, strong Italian coffee was good. While we were there, this little girl, kept peeking around the corner of the counter at us. She couldn't have been over 3 years old. Finally, I walked over toward her and gave her mother a chocolate bar for her. That little girl's smile warmed us up more than the coffee. And she warmed up to us too. We found out her name was Paola and by the time we left, she had all of our chocolate bars! The friendliness of Paola's family at the restaurant made us glad we had stopped in. As we were heading back down the mountain in the jeep, I couldn't help but think of home and especially Carol. She would be about the same age a Paola. I hope she hasn't forgotten me since I've been gone.

116

Paola Sozzi with an American
soldier outside her family's Futa
Pass restaurant in late 1944.
Photo courtesy of Paola's son Claudio Poletti

21 Nov 1944

A group of us went to Florence yesterday. It is a pretty amazing place, even with the war damage – which is actually minimal compared to a place like Naples. Even though the Germans retreated from Rome to Florence, the Allies realized that Florence held too much historic art & buildings to sustain heavy bombing or artillery attacks. We bombed the train station, which cut off the Nazi's supply lines and eventually forced them to leave. Before they did they destroyed most of the city's historic bridges over the Arno in an attempt to slow down our advance. The only bridge they left standing is the Ponte Vecchio bridge, which we saw yesterday. It was worth seeing. I don't know much about art, but I'm glad we didn't bomb Florence.

23 Nov 1944

Thanksgiving Day and I am thankful tonight! Last night, we were informed that C Battery was scheduled to go to the new Fifth Army Rest Center at Montecatini west of Florence. This morning we loaded up in trucks and off we went. I think we will be here a couple of more days. We had a nice supper tonight and we are staying in a hotel room. I'm feeling better than I have in weeks. We are well out of harm's way here.

This place has a hot springs and apparently was a popular place for wealthy Italians before the war. It is the nicest place I've been. I wrote Mildred tonight and told her all about it. I hope she has had a good Thanksgiving with her family. I plan on being with her next year for Thanksgiving.

I'm thankful to be alive after my close call last month and I am thankful to be at this place right now.

25 Nov 1944

I'm really enjoying the hot showers, clean uniforms and hot meals here. We sleep on cots, without shoes, or outer clothing in a warm room under a dry blanket!

Visited the ancient Roman baths here and have been able to do some reading. There are movies, haircuts, laundry, and shoe shines – it is like a resort. I was able to get some new socks here too.

26 Nov 1944

Life here is almost too good to believe. Clean beds & rooms, hot meals, baths, movies, USO shows, restaurants, and bars. Some of the boys might be enjoying a little too much (in the bars anyway) but it is a well-earned time for all. We still have a six-hour daily drill schedule and section training for the battery, but after that, the free time is almost too good to be true.

Even though we all know we are headed back to the front soon, this time at the rest camp has really helped us all feel better.

1 Dec 1944

We left Montecantini a couple of days ago and we are back in our bivouac/training area near Gagliano. Morale is high after our time in the rest area. We continue to train & march every day, as well as work to maintain the guns & equipment. Looks like the winter weather has stalled any advance toward Bologna until spring. Our days here aren't very exciting, but I believe the men like it that way. Most of us have had more excitement in Italy than we ever wanted anyway.

5 Dec 1944

Everybody at home has been real good about writing. When we can get mail, it seems like I get something about every week. Daddy, Geraldine, Mildred, Aunt Flossie, and some of Momma's sisters sometime. Then there are folks from Notasulga who write to all the local boys overseas. My letter today was from Aunt Crecie. She said Doug was doing fine in the Marines and was somewhere in the Pacific. Aunt Crecie has always been one of my favorites and one of the best cooks in Lee County. I sure would like to sit down at her table tonight! I appreciate everybody writing. I know by the time the V-mail gets here it is out of date, but it still makes me feel good to hear from home. I always try to answer their letters with a note too.

11 Dec 1944

Passes to Florence are readily available to all of us now. I will probably go back down there for a day, but I'm pretty content to remain here in bivouac right now. Life out here without being fired upon daily is okay with me. Its cold up here, but the cold weather conditions are what is keeping us from fighting right now, so I'm not complaining.

18 Dec 1944

Most mornings here, there is usually a misty fog that hangs low, almost into midday, which makes it difficult to see very far sometimes. This has to be hard on the boys on the front line, but at least things are sort of at a standstill there.

Even with the fog and cold weather, I like the mornings here. You can usually hear a rooster crow which reminds me of home. With Christmas approaching, our thoughts turn to home quite often. We all hope this will be our last Christmas away from home. We live for the letters and parcels from home. Everybody at home has been really faithful in writing to me. It really helps the boys' morale here when they hear from home.

20 Dec 1944

We heard that the Germans have mounted an unexpected big offensive in Belgium that caught our troops off guard and have cut off thousands of our soldiers. The fact that they were willing to do this in such bad weather makes us all a little uneasy here. There are stories that they are shooting captured American soldiers. It doesn't sound good.

22 Dec 1944

With Christmas approaching, the men are tense, wondering if the Germans might try something here in Italy like they have on the Western Front. From what we hear, our soldiers were completely surprised there and casualties are high. They are totally surrounded and bad weather is keeping the Allies from helping them out. Lots of GIs in a bad situation. There are German soldiers dressed in American uniforms who speak English that are infiltrating American positions there too. We've been warned of the possibility of that happening here.

With all of this on our mind, some of us are still planning to decorate a big tree to invite the local Italian children over on Christmas Day. We don't have much in the way of gifts for them, but some of the boys have made things and we have some chocolate bars. It will be good to share a little Christmas with children.

23 Dec 1944

Last night we were alerted for a move. This morning we moved out in convoy headed west through Florence, Pistoia, and Lucca to the Western Coastal Sector. As we had feared, it seems the Germans are threatening some type of activity over here. We are bivouacked just north of Lucca in support of the 92nd Division. From our position, we can see the rugged mountains a few miles north of us where the German's are dug in.

I'm sorry we won't get to do our Christmas with the children near Gagliano, but we left the things we had planned to give them there so they can have them on Christmas Day.

Chow time for the some of the 328th FA near Lucca in late December, 1944.
Photo courtesy of Steve Cole, son of Sgt. Newton F. Cole, Battery B, 328th FA

24 Dec 1944

Christmas Eve.   We are on alert, but it is hard not to think of home and the people you miss.

After a prayer service, we sang some Christmas carols.   We prayed for lots of things silently and as a group.   The chaplain led us all in a prayer for the boys in the Ardennes Forest.   Sounds like they have it bad with lots of casualties.

We listened to the radio some tonight.   Axis Sally always plays some good big band music for us, but tonight she is playing Christmas music.   Even with her telling us we need to surrender and how bad we are doing, we still like listening to her.   Can't beat Bing Crosby singing White Christmas, even if it does make you homesick.

Some of the boys got to talking about Christmas with their families when they were growing up.   Somebody would tell a funny story, then someone else, and then it would get quite.   You could tell everybody was thinking about home.   Then someone else would pipe up with a tale.   If I can't be home for Christmas, then there is nowhere else I would rather be than with these boys. Good men.

25 Dec 1944

Christmas night and we are on a three hour alert. We have been able to settle into farm buildings north of town and are ready to move if needed. In spite of this, we have actually had a very nice Christmas. Don't know how the cooks came up with all the rations. We had turkey & dressing with cranberry sauce and all the trimmings – sweet potatoes, gravy, peas, chocolate cake & raisin bread! For those who wanted it there were cigars, cigarettes, and white wine. The cooks really outdid themselves today.

The Red Cross gave each of us a gift package which had a bag of hard candy, a bag of chocolates, an address book, a comb and some other small items. It was really nice and made everybody feel good.

We managed to enjoy some of the spirit of Christmas, by inviting some of the locals to join our chow line. We were able to share some of the candy and things we had with the Italian children. Their gratitude and smiles made it a great Christmas for us.

27 Dec 1944

Yesterday was pretty tense as our alert was shortened to thirty minutes and we were expecting to move all day. All our trucks were loaded and guns prepared, ready to pull out. Two brigades of the Indian 8th Infantry have already moved north to help the 92nd. Sounds like the Germans are gaining ground in the Serchio Valley and headed south toward us.

Tonight, the alert has been relaxed to one hour. I will settle in and try to get some sleep, but it wouldn't surprise me if we move out tonight.

30 Dec 1944

It's been a busy few days with tensions high. We pulled out of our position north of Lucca at 2300 hours on the night of the 27th. We moved north and northwest through one set of mountains through Viareggio into position near Motrone.

After setting up position there, the next night we were moving again, this time back toward the coast near Viareggio. When the sun came up we could see the beautiful coastal plain and the mountains to the north & east looking down on us. While beautiful, there wasn't much comfort because we knew we were under observation. We had our 105s set up and we fired our first round in over a month when registration started that morning. There were no fire missions, though since the Germans made no threatening moves that day.

Tonight we have moved into positions just southeast of Camaiore near the coast. The Germans have made a hard push on the 92nd. The front lines are just within maximum range of our guns. But we haven't fired as of now. Our mission is to cover the withdrawal of the 92nd in case of a breakthrough.

The weather is nice here. It's a lot warmer near the coast here in the west. The temperate climate surprised us all after what we've seen in the Apennines. This would be a good area to spend the rest of the winter as far as I'm concerned.

This anti-tank wall, part of the Gothic Line north of Lucca, was constructed by the Germans using local slave labor. Photograph taken in 2014.

1 Jan 1945

Happy New Year. We started the New Year pretty much like all our days have started lately – with a move to a new position. At 0645 this morning, we moved about a mile to the northwest, closing into position in the vicinity of Servagliana.   No time for festivities as we got in position, dug in, and completed registration on our guns. We are ready if anything happens.

Actually, it's not too bad here. The buildings are pretty much untouched and we have running water.   We fired a few harassing missions earlier tonight, but most of the activity is beyond our range.

Another new year. You have to wonder what this one will bring. I remember being on the ship last New Year's Day, before we landed at Casablanca. '44 was a tough year, one I'll never be able to forget. We all thought the war would be over by now. Hopefully 1945 will see the end of it and I make it back to Notasulga safe and sound. That's my prayer tonight.

10 Jan 1945

No more nice weather -- we're back in the central Apennines tonight. Icy, dreary & cold with snow on the ground. I don't like these mountains. We left the Western Coastal Sector a couple of days ago and are back in the front lines north of Florence. We have relieved the British and the 337th Infantry has completely reoccupied its former positions on Montecalderaro and Cuccoli ridge now. Cold days ahead. I'm glad I still have my old combat jacket with the wool collar & cuffs – I think it is warmer than the new field jacket. Plus, I can wear it under the new jacket if needed.

14 Jan 1945

Things are a lot more active for us here. We are firing harassing missions, but observed missions are few because of the poor visibility. With supplies short, we still have some ammo restrictions.

Last night a German patrol entered our lines and took one of our boys prisoner. One of the Germans was killed as they escaped, but they still had our man. We have to be careful on the radio too. It seems like they have our frequencies. Everything is pretty tense right now. They seem to be stepping up their activities against us here.

20 Jan 1945

We took some heavy shelling this morning. Probably the worst we've had in a couple of months. One of the guys in B Battery was wounded as well as 3 of the Brits who are up here. We've been using smoke to conceal our activity here, but high winds this morning helped expose us and gave the enemy an opportunity to hit us.

Even when we aren't being shelled or shot at, accidental casualties can take a serious toll. A couple of days ago, a rifleman came back from a patrol mission and in his hurry to get in line for hot coffee he forgot to put the safety pin back in the rifle grenade hanging on his belt. As he was getting in the line, somehow the grenade fell to the ground and went off. It wounded 14 boys who had to be evacuated, including some of the cooks.

We heard that the Allies have been able to break out in the Bulge and have launched an offensive that has the Germans pulling back. Sounds like it was a bad month there – something like 18,000 Americans killed.

24 Jan 1945

Yesterday and today were clear & sunny days – a good change. Still cold, but the sun makes everybody feel better.

We've got a good position here on high ground. With the clearer weather yesterday, our observers have been able to spot several small groups of enemy soldiers out just walking around, doing chores like they don't care if we see them or not. We fired a few missions to let them know we saw them and they moved back underground. I guess they wanted to get out and enjoy the clear weather as well.

Lt. Darnell (front row, far right) with some members of Battery C in the Apennine Mountains north of Florence in 1945.
Photo courtesy of Bill Dempsey

26 Jan 1945

The last couple of days we've been maintaining our current position as well as preparing a rear position in case of German counter-attack that would force us to withdraw from where we are now. It seems like right now everything is a stalemate, with occasional small moves on either side, but nothing big can happen because of the weather. But we remember how the Germans surprised our soldiers at the Battle of the Bulge just a few weeks ago in bad weather, so we have to be ready. These mountains are a tough place to be in January, much less try to move and fight. The boys carry on despite the stinging wind that freezes your face and blurs your vision.

It's cold, but for the most part we have plenty of clothes. The wool uniforms and socks really do a good job. We've been issued zip up sleeping bags that are warm, but most of us just use our GI blankets. Too hard to get out of the zip up bag if you have to fight in a hurry. Some of the boys are calling them "Purple Heart Bags" because if the Germans counter-attack you could get bayonetted before you ever got out of the bag.

30 Jan 1945

We've completed our rear positions in case we have to fall back in a hurry. Been firing a few observed and harassing missions which are pretty regular now – just to let the Germans know we still care.

We fired some rounds using the new VT fuse a couple of nights ago when one of our observers noticed some unusual enemy activity. First time we had fired any of them. They explode several feet off the ground and are designed to take out personnel more than anything else. If they work like we've been told, they will be a very deadly weapon. We will find out.

*Battery C commander Capt. William Dempsey (left), and Lt. Darnell (center)
shown with one of the 105s during winter 1945.*
Photo courtesy of Bill Dempsey

5 Feb 1945

Activity in our area is picking up. This morning we fired some concentrations on our left sector to support a move by the 34th Infantry Division.   The most firing we've done in a few weeks. The move was successful as the 34th shored up the flank with their gains in that area.

Got a letter from Lucille yesterday.   I wrote her back today and told her that when I get home, I am going to see Mildred, and I won't be writing to her anymore.   Lucille is a good girl, but Mildred is the one I want to be with.   Things that have happened the last few months have made me realize that.   There were times when I didn't know if I was going to make it and Mildred was the one on my mind. She is the one for me.   I wrote Mildred tonight and told her how much she means to me.   As soon as I get home, I am going to see her and tell her face to face how I feel.

13 Feb 1945

Received an order today to be on alert for unusual signs of enemy activity. There is information that the Germans might try something big here. So far, we haven't noticed anything out of the ordinary, but everybody is on their toes.

19 Feb 1945

Last night we were firing some preparation for a combat patrol that was going out to try to get a prisoner. As we were firing, apparently, one of our sentries was walking the line and someone tapped him on the shoulder. He turned around to find a German soldier who wanted to surrender. How that German got through the mine field and that close to our sentry is a mystery. Needless to say, the number of sentries & their alertness increased after that. The patrol was called off since we had a prisoner now.

I saw the German prisoner and he looked bad -- thin like he hadn't had much to eat. His uniform was in rough shape. Looks like it's worse for them up here than it is for us. Maybe they will all give up before spring. That would save lots of lives.

Lt. Darnell (far right, front) with other artillerymen from the 328th FA.
Photo courtesy of Steve Cole

23 Feb 1945

A couple of days ago, the HQ of the 1st Battalion of the 337th received a direct hit from a mortar shell which killed the Battalion commander and four other soldiers. Several boys were wounded. I knew all these men – had been in the middle of it with several of them. Capt. Dempsey, was in the HQ and said he walked out only minutes before the shell hit.

We've been pretty busy with some observed fire the last couple of days. Our FO spotted a couple of tanks and we got a direct hit on one, even though the other one got away. Then yesterday he adjusted our fire as we took out an enemy gun emplacement. When the Germans in it ran to another bunker, he directed us as we got a hit on that one and caved it in too. We stopped firing when work parties came to dig them out with a Red Cross flag. One minute, we're killing people and the next we're letting them be rescued. Sometimes this war doesn't make sense.

27 Feb 1945

We've been out patrolling around our position area the last couple of days. We got word that the Germans have some long-range patrols operating behind our lines, so we've been taking a patrol out every few hours to try and find them. Patrolling in this area is dangerous because, due to the snow & terrain, there are just a few suitable routes. If there are Germans behind our lines, it would be fairly easy for them to set an ambush. We try to vary our patrol route as much as possible, but our options are limited. So far, nothing, but the men are on their alert.

Except for that concern, we have made our position here as secure as possible. We are well dug in and have decent protection from both shell and weather.

4 Mar 1945

We continue to be harassed daily by German artillery, including one of their big 210 mm guns. Those are their biggest guns they've ever fired at us. The distinct sound of those big shells coming in is hard to forget. We also continue to maintain a smoke screen to reduce the enemy observation of our positions. The smoke is aggravating to us after a while, but it is better than being shot or shelled.

We return the favor most nights and when our FO spots targets, we go after them. We have fired on some dugouts & buildings and a couple of self-propelled guns, but good targets here are hard to find right now.

9 Mar 1945

Yesterday, all of the 85th Division except the 328th received orders to be relieved. So today, we remain in position while the rest of the Division has moved back out of the line. They were relieved by the 10th Indian Division, so we are in support of them at the moment. We've worked with the 10th Indian before – good soldiers.

105mm howitzer crew with gun in 1945. Lt. Darnell is on back row, far right.
Photo courtesy of Bill Dempsey.

15 Mar 1945

Still in position, but we are now attached to the 97th Kent Yeoman Regiment Royal Artillery, under their control. We are using both our own and British observers to adjust our fire. There are some terminology differences between us and the British artillery that we have to get used to, but it's not too difficult. Always interesting to be around soldiers from other countries, but I would rather be under Division control.

22 Mar 1945

Tonight we are back in our old bivouac area near Gagliano, north of Florence, after spending the last ten weeks in the line. We were relieved on the 20th and moved back here. We haven't been here since we left to go to Lucca right before Christmas. It is familiar and beats living in the dugouts on the line.

Despite the enemy still looking aggressive and determined, it seems to me that there are indications that the war is winding down. The noises the Germans make seem out of proportion to what they actually do sometimes. When they hit us, they don't follow through like they always have in the past. Seems more and more like harassment and less like trying to hold or gain ground. I'm hoping the spring offensive will finish off the war in Italy. I also know that some of us won't make it through to see the end of it. We all know our number can come up at any time.

We received a new shoe here called a "shoe pac". Supposed to be better for winter. It's like a boot with a rubber bottom part & leather top. We'll see how it works out.

24 Mar 1945

Today we made an 8 hr convoy trip and tonight we are near Pisa for river crossing training. Even when we are in reserve, we always continue to train or run some type of attack problem. This is important for a lot of reasons, but it is necessary because replacements need to get experience working with the more experienced men in the units. Any successful assault depends on each man knowing what is expected of him and doing it. There isn't much time to learn under fire. In addition it is good for the new men to get to know the other men in their units. Working on these exercises together allows for that too. It is a sad time when one of the new men gets killed and nobody even knows his name.

28 Mar 1945

We left Pisa and last night we moved into our new position in the line. Looks like things are happening in preparation for the spring offensive we've been anticipating. Our ammo stocks are plentiful – the largest they've been in quite some time. Our Battery allotment is about 500 rounds per day and we have orders to fire them. There isn't a lot of observed targets but we are doing a good bit of unobserved shoots on suspected positions and have increased our harassing missions. Definitely starting to soften up the enemy lines. So far, we haven't had a single incoming shell either – so that is good. However, the main road from Loiano to the battalion area is under German observation and they are shelling it regularly.

Lt. Darnell (front, center) with soldiers from Battery C

30 Mar 1945

Today is Good Friday. If the weather is suitable back home, I know Daddy is working his garden today.

Got a letter from Geraldine. She has met a Coast Guard sailor in Washington that she really likes. They've been going out a lot and it is beginning to sound serious. He must be a good guy to be able to put up with her! Seriously, I'm glad she met someone who makes her feel special. Makes me think of Mildred and how much I want to be that man for her.

Think I am going back to my old shoes & leggings. The shoe pac is a good idea to try to keep our feet dry, but it doesn't seem to give much support for the foot. Over long distances, they will kill your feet. Plus they seem to be slippery. Some of the guys have wrapped them in burlap from sand bags to keep from slipping when they wear them. As long as I can keep a pair of dry socks, I can do okay with the old shoes.

1 Apr 1945

It is a sunny Easter Sunday and we are still in position.

I am thankful that I had a mother who had a strong faith. When I was little, she prayed and read the Bible with me every day. Even with her health problems, she was strong and her faith made her stronger. I don't know if I could make it here without my faith. You hear a lot about how tough soldiers are (and these boys are), but when it comes down to it, everybody here prays. One of the chaplains came by the Battery this morning and we had a sunrise service by the guns. I appreciated him doing that. It was a peaceful day overall with not much firing going on.

One of many Easter services held on Apennine mountainsides on April 1, 1945. This one is with men of the 10th Mountain Division. Photo by Roy O. Bingham

Photo of Battery A, 328th FA taken near Ramagnola in 1945. Photo was snapped at the instance two guns fired. Emplacements for four guns are shown in the photo. Photo courtesy of Alan Biggs, son of Major George Biggs, XO of 328th FA

CHAPTER FIFTEEN
SPRING AND THE FINAL PUSH

6 Apr 1945

We moved west again, this time into bivouac with the rest of the 85th Division near the town of Lecci. They must be getting ready to move us into position somewhere else though because a lot of things are happening. Weather is beginning to break and lots of movement right now. More and more of our bombers are flying over headed north every day. Appears the Spring Offensive is close.

10 Apr 1945

Last night we moved into our new position near Abba. It was quite a move over treacherous mountain roads in a complete blackout. No mishaps though and we spent today digging in and preparing positions. We are currently detached from the 85th Infantry Division and assigned to support part of the 10th Mountain Division artillery. The 85th is in reserve right now, but we will be moving with the 10th when the assault begins.

15 Apr 1945

We had two 24-hour postponements, but we finally began our fire missions for the offensive yesterday morning. After 35 minutes of hard artillery fire and strong air bombardment of

139

German positions the infantry moved forward and were able to capture most of the German positions on the ridges north of us. Heavy casualties among the enemy and we have captured lots of prisoners at this point.

Soldiers of Battery C, 328th FA, in the Apennine mud in spring, 1945. Capt. Dempsey is on first row, fourth from left. Lt. Darnell is on second row, far left.
Photo courtesy of Bill Dempsey

17 Apr 1945

I have to say, those boys with the 10th Mountain Division infantry are something else. I heard most of them grew up in the mountains out west, skiing and climbing mountains. I believe it. They move fast and hard in this rough terrain. By yesterday morning they had taken all the high ground to the north of our position including the big Mt. Pero. With them seizing this high ground, it was time for us to move to the next valley and re-position. Tonight we are in position near Cereglio after a

140

difficult move along the only usable road. The road was along a steep cliff and was a mess. Not only was it narrow and muddy, it was jammed with vehicles and supplies moving forward as everyone was on the move. We got into position last night, but A Battery didn't get here until 0400 this morning. Luckily the Germans are retreating in disarray and couldn't take advantage of this situation.

18 Apr 1945

Seems like the Germans have recovered somewhat from the initial attack and are giving it back to us now. Their self-propelled guns are hitting all our northward approaches hard. We anticipated this, but it has slowed us down some. We were still able to displace forward this afternoon with some casualties. Our batteries remained close behind the leading elements and were always in a position to deliver fire as needed. Moving and firing.

20 Apr 1945

We have reverted back to control of the 85th and in support of the 337th. The last couple of days we have made two successive jumps to Borra and then to Bell'Aria, which puts us in the last hills before the Po Valley. At Borra, the Germans left a whole battery of camouflaged 105s and their half-eaten meal. I don't think they expected us to be moving this fast. The Po Valley has been our objective since last fall and we're getting close.

Some recon teams have reached the valley but ran into some stiff resistance in the town of Casalecchio. We have been firing volleys about as fast as we can into the town tonight, in preparation for the 6th South African Division's entry into the town.

21 Apr 1945

We finally entered the Po Valley today and are in position near Highway 9 at Anzola dell'Emilia. It is a great relief to be here and know that the enemy is no longer able to look down on our every move. The mountains of the Gothic Line are behind us and the flat plains of the Po before us.

Things are really moving fast, but we've got to be careful. Whenever we move, minefields are a big concern, especially if you get off the road and into fields like in this valley. The Germans have mined behind them as they retreated all the way through Italy. Our Engineers usually have swept a path through minefields for us to follow and mark the perimeter with white tape. But we are moving fast now and sometimes artillery or bombing has cut the strips of tape making the exact path hard to determine. These mines are bad things. The Germans have two main types we have run across: the shoe mine & the Bouncing Betty. The shoe mines are usually put in a wooden box which makes them harder to detect with a mine detector. If you step on one of these, it will blow off your foot. The Bouncing Betty is even deadlier. When you step on a trigger for one of these, it blows a canister about 4-5 feet in the air and then explodes, spreading shrapnel over a large area. Those have killed and wounded lots of men since we've been here.

23 Apr 1945

The spring rains stopped several days ago and the weather has warmed up. The roads and open, flat land here are solid. No dense trees, mountains, or hills to obstruct our visibility or slow us down. Things are moving so fast now, that we are concerned about being bombed by our own airplanes. The last couple of days, all of our vehicles have had bright pink and orange ID panels painted on top of them so the airmen won't attack them. There have been some instances of casualties from friendly fire in other units.

24 Apr 1945

We are making rapid moves every day now. The advantage is ours and the resistance is disorganized. This open country allows our air power to be more effective against the retreating Germans.

Yesterday morning we approached the Po River and were moving our guns into firing position about 1500 meters short of the river to support the crossing by our infantry. As we were getting into position, we ran up on a large group of Germans who started dropping their weapons as we approached. It was a little touchy, since there were as many of them as there were of us. Captain Dempsey was at HQ, so I was the CO in his absence. As we held our weapons on them, I spotted a German officer and moved toward him. It was then I noticed he was an SS Colonel. In pretty good English, he asked to see the commanding officer to surrender. I told him that was me. At that point he shouted something in German out to the German soldiers. The Colonel, then unbuckled his holster and handed me his pistol with great show. I had never seen a Luger quite like that one – it was chrome plated and shiny. Of course I had never seen a live SS Colonel up close either. The German told me it had been presented to him by Hitler himself. I don't know if that is true, but it is a nice gun, and a good story.

There were 89 Germans in that group that surrendered. And I kept the Colonel's gun.

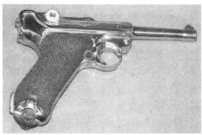

Luger taken from SS Colonel

After that bit of excitement we had some infantry boys move the prisoners back toward the rear and we got our guns set up for the crossing.

This morning we began firing our preparation at 0530 and the first wave of soldiers crossed the Po at 0545 in assault boats with no opposition from the northern bank. The rest of the morning was spent with the infantry crossing.

We later fired on several enemy tanks and targets of opportunity, but the crossing went about as good as could be expected.

Tonight we are still on the south side of the river, in position, awaiting our orders to move across. There are no bridges in our sector, but the engineers are working on a temporary bridge to get our equipment across when the time comes.

We have to be close to German surrender – they are on the run and disorganized now. We've heard that Hitler called on all German citizens to fight to the death as the Allies move through Germany. Most of their soldiers here aren't following that order. They've abandoned trucks, jeeps, and other equipment here on the south side of the Po as they crossed the river in a hurry. They even left some of their draft horses here and crossed without them. Farmers have been coming out and gathering them up and taking them to their farms.

26 Apr 1945

We moved into position here near Zera about 0130 this morning after crossing the Po yesterday. Our river crossing training in Pisa had been specifically for this purpose as we crossed on a bridge of rubber boats. No major incidents in the crossing but it was slow and tedious.

Last night the Germans bombed and shelled the bridge, but luckily we were far enough away, it didn't affect us.

28 Apr 1945

As we moved forward across the plains of the Po Valley, we were greeted by Italians – men, women, and children – who were coming out to greet us with cheers, wine, fresh eggs, cheese, flowers, and kisses. It has been a while since we have seen anything like this. It is remarkable to see and makes everybody feel better. This valley has been our objective since last fall, so it is good to be here finally.

29 Apr 1945

It is Sunday night and tonight we are on the outskirts of Verona. Verona is a big rail center for northern Italy and just south of the Brenner Pass – the way to southern Germany. Our bombers have pretty much destroyed the big rail yard here. We have spotted German positions on the high ground overlooking our position, but there aren't firing on us. While there is small resistance, most are surrendering as we encounter them. All units have been really moving fast. This is different from our previous advances. The infantry boys are riding on tanks & trucks as they advance, instead of on foot.

We're taking prisoners in droves now. It's easy to forget sometimes that most of the regular German soldiers (not the SS) are just like us – they have family at home and the most important thing to them is to get back home and see them. One of the prisoners we took today spoke English and told us that before the war he had lived in Berlin where he was a store clerk. He had been drafted, just like so many of our boys. We couldn't talk to him very long before he was taken away, but you realize that this war has been hard on everybody. The sooner it is over, the better.

30 Apr 1945

We got orders to move eastward toward Venice today, but plans changed before we ever got there. Tonight we are in an assembly area at Creazzo near Vicenza. In spite of the multiple moves and some seeming confusion, morale is high. Everybody knows that victory is close, but there are still firefights & German resistance to our advances. The enemy is getting desperate, so anything can happen. I've got to make sure Battery C stays on their toes, because I sure don't want to lose anyone this close to what we hope is the end.

1 May 1945

We have moved well beyond the Po Valley now and into the Italian Alps. Yesterday was a long move that put us in the vicinity of Pederobba and then to Anzu. We are standing by in support of the infantry as they clear towns ahead of us. We have heard a rumor that Hitler committed suicide -- we are all hoping that will speed up the end of this.

CHAPTER SIXTEEN
THE GERMAN ARMY SURRENDERS

2 May 1945

The German Army in Italy surrendered today! Everyone here is smiling and feeling relieved, but there is still disbelief and some confusion. It is hard to describe the feeling because we have been going so hard for so long that it doesn't seem real.

The day started out fighting though. We had advanced to Gron in support of an armored task force, heading toward one of the Alpine Passes into Austria and began to encounter trouble. About 1230, we ran up on the tail end of a retreating German division on the narrow mountain road. A short firefight ensued with some of our GIs on the lead tanks being killed. A truce was called to discuss surrender, but the Germans wanted to keep their small arms. Our boys couldn't let them do that so fighting erupted again. Finally seeing they had no other option, the German column surrendered unconditionally and all their weapons were tossed off the road into a deep ravine.

Rumor had it that all the German armies in Italy were surrendering, but we didn't receive official word of the surrender until late in the afternoon. We were ordered to halt in place.

We are alert and in our firing position. Tonight, I am so thankful that it looks like our fighting is over, but I can't stop thinking about those poor boys who were killed this afternoon in that firefight, so close to the end of all of this.

3 May 1945

We remain in position in Gron.   Hundreds of German prisoners are streaming through here and are being sent back to the POW enclosures.   These poor guys look beaten and half-starved. Apparently we did a good job cutting off their supply lines. One of our guys here who speaks German said he talked with a couple of the German prisoners and they are as glad it is over as we are. All they want to do is go home.   I know that feeling.

The surrender in Italy is the largest-scale enemy capitulation of the war so far.   Hopefully this will lead to surrender throughout Europe soon.

Today, we remained alert and in position for firing.   The infantry is mopping up German units and many are still armed. Even though they have surrendered it can still be dangerous.

It seems like most of the boys are still in disbelief that this may finally be over, although Germany hasn't surrendered totally yet. There is talk that our next move may be to push on through the Alps and into Germany.

5 May 1945

It is looking like we may be here for some time.   We received training orders yesterday – three hours of drill and maintenance in the morning and three hours of recreation and athletics in the afternoon.   Sounds like a transition from combat.   I have to say the schedule was a little bit of a surprise and I'm hoping it is proof that the fighting has ceased.   We have heard that negotiations are underway for Germany's complete surrender.

The only movement in our Division was yesterday when the 339th moved up to seal the Austrian border. We are assisting the 337th in gathering together and evacuating surrendered units in our zone.

I traded one of the boys in the 337th for a nice camera he took off of a German officer. Now I need to figure out how to use it.

Lt. Darnell's German camera and case.

9 May 1945

The war in Europe is over! We got word that Germany officially surrendered. Words can't really describe how I feel right now. Disbelief that it is finally over. Relief that we don't have to fight on to Germany. Thankful that I'm alive.

All the boys were whooping and hollering when we got the news. Our CO had to remind everyone that we still had a job to do here and that it is still dangerous, but what a great day! Everybody is thinking about getting home as soon as possible.

10 May 1945

It's different around right now. We're taking German prisoners by the droves. After 3 weeks of fast moves, we're holding tight here for now.

Captured German vehicles are everywhere. Trucks, cars, motorcycles, even horses. After months of walking, lots of soldiers are using these to get around now. They paint a white star on them and load up. We saw one of the infantrymen driving a captured Buick. He pulled up with a couple of buddies and the German colonel he had taken the car from. He turned his prisoner in and then he and his buddies jumped back in the car and left to go back to their unit.

11 May 1945

The 328th was released from combat team control yesterday and moved to our new area of responsibility. HQ was set up at Lentiai. Our responsibility is to occupy and patrol this area. We're working with the Italian partisans in clearing out the scattered Germans hiding in the hills. A lot of the Germans have gotten rid of their uniforms and are just trying to get back to Germany without being taken prisoner. The Italian partisans' considerable help in northern Italy has earned our respect.

It was one year ago today that we jumped off against the Gustav Line near Minturno in our first major offensive. It's been a long year, but the fighting is finally over.

Front page of Vol. 1, No. 1 of the 328th FA newspaper published in Italy on May 11, 1945. Lt. Darnell's handwritten note and signature are at the top where he sent it home with instructions "Keep this for me".

Lt. Darnell, somewhere in Italy, 1945.

13 May 1945

Today is Mother's Day. All the boys are writing home and telling their mothers that they should be home soon. Guess I will never not miss Momma and that's the way it should be. It would sure be great to talk with her and tell her about the things that have happened over here.

I enjoyed church today. The chaplain mentioned that the 328th had endured 402 days in combat and traveled over 1000 miles from Minturno to our present location in the Alps.

15 May 1945

I heard today that some of the boys in the 339th found $15,000,000 worth of Nazi gold in the Alps near the Austrian border. I wonder what that much gold looks like. There's no telling what the Nazis have hidden away.

I read that the 328th has fought with 10 different Allied Divisions in Italy, not counting our own 85th Infantry Division. Included in that was British, South African, and Indian divisions.

16 May 1945

The last few days our routine patrols have picked up a few scattered Germans in civilian clothes, trying to sneak through here and make it back to Germany. Even though the war is over, these patrols can still be dangerous because some of these men are armed and desperate to get back to Germany. We have to be careful with everyone we approach. The partisans on patrol with us are of great help.

All the boys are talking about what they are going to do when they get home. I know the first thing I want to do is go see Mildred. I think about her more than anything else. We are all excited, but in the back of our minds there is apprehension that we might get sent to the Pacific if the Japanese don't surrender soon.

19 May 1945

Got a letter from Daddy today. Carl has been wounded. Got some type of head wound fighting on one of those islands. Sounds like his platoon caught it bad & he is lucky to be alive. Not a lot of details about what happened, but at least he is alive. Even though things seem to be winding down here, Daddy will be lucky if both his sons make it home from this war in one piece.

22 May 1945

Our schedule remains pretty much the same. We continue to round up German soldiers. While there have been some tense moments, so far, none of our men have been hurt doing this. German officers really don't like to surrender to enlisted men. Most days we take from one to six prisoners, although on the 18th we had a busy day, picking up 39 Germans. As we gather up the prisoners, we send them on to the 339th who is responsible for processing and evacuating the prisoners from the Division's zone. Most of the time the German officers are helpful in controlling their men, although some are pretty arrogant and think the GIs should salute them. They find out pretty quick that doesn't happen.

The partisans helping us are a good group. They all fought in the resistance and hate the fascists of Mussolini as bad as they hate the Germans. While they work well with us, they are a hard bunch. They have all lost family members in this war and most have lost their homes. They appreciate what we've done over here, but I get the feeling they just want their country and lives back.

CUSTER COMBATEER

VOL. I NO. 3 • 85TH DIV. CD IN ITALY • MAY 1945

DAYS TO REMEMBER:

May 2, 1945

SURRENDER IN ITALY

May 8, 1945

VICTORY IN EUROPE

85th Division Helps Shatter Wehrmacht

The Nazi state has disappeared in dust and shame. All over Europe German army commanders, having seen the example of their beaten comrades in Italy, hastened to lay down their arms in the greatest military debacle of all time. History was made, and the 85th Custer Division helped make it by a great sweep from the Apennines to the Alps.

It's the story of 16 days which the men of the 85th will long remember. The Division pushed off on April 17.... Over the peaks and down into the valley at last.... Across Highway 9.... On to the Po River.... Across the water barrier.... Then swiftly north towards .... and ....

The advance was swift and spectacular. Taken by surprise, enemy defenses years in construction crumbled in hours. The Division which had broken through

the Gustav Line and had cracked the Gothic Line, only after bitter struggles, found these new lines a different story. Genghis Khan, Barbara, Dottie, Adige— our men swept through one defense line after another.

.... forced marches. Some doughboys rode Recon vehicles, tanks, Jerry vehicles, and even captured German horses. One of our men, driving a captured Buick with the German Colonel from

whom he had taken it beside him, said it was the first American car he'd driven since '42 and it was like a real touch of home. The doughboy soon turned his prisoner in but the Buick carried him and his buddies for many a dusty mile. Everywhere along the roads of the advance our convoys were spotted with an assortment of Jerry trucks, command cars, sedans,—white stars hastily painted on them but still bearing Wehrmacht license plates.

Two 339th Infantry .... Jerry Captain on a m........ right into their fox-hole........ guns spoke. The .... without ......

The 337th's 3rd Battalion found a good ration supplement when a Fritzie Bakery was captured—bread still warm

(Continued on last page.)

Flushing Out Jerries

27 May 1945

We received notice today from Division that we are scheduled to be relieved shortly from our present duties. The Folgore Group will be taking over for us. I've heard of them before. They are a combat unit made up of Italians that wear British uniforms. I'm glad they will be taking over here. I will be happy if I never see another German soldier.

Hopefully we will be headed back south and out of Italy soon!

30 May 1945

Yesterday the entire battalion moved into an assembly area with the rest of the Division Artillery. Tonight we are in the vicinity of Pez. Today the schedule of training and recreation was re-instituted. The morale of the men is extremely high and they are enjoying peace time and the prospects of heading home. We listen closely for news of the war with Japan. There is a lingering concern in the mind of some (especially the newer guys) that instead of going home, they could be headed to fight in the Pacific. We all are hoping that they surrender soon. Most everybody here has family or friends who are fighting the Japanese.

3 June 1945

Looks like I'm going to get to use my degree some while I'm here. The Army has authorized the establishment of a school for the men teaching limited subjects while we are here awaiting our next move (hopefully home). One of the subjects is Agriculture, so I am one of the instructors for that. Over 300 men signed up for the 12 subjects offered. That will be good experience for me.

In addition to the classes, we continue to do a light training program and athletic activities, including softball. My pitching is getting better so maybe we will be able to finally beat Headquarters Battery.

9 June 1945

The entire Division has been put on alert for a possible move to a new sector in the vicinity of Trieste, near the Yugoslavian border. There has been some trouble there between the Yugoslavian Army and the other Allied occupying forces.

156

Even with an impending move, softball is going full blast. HQ Battery is still the best team, but we all have fun. The Battalion has put together a team from all the batteries to represent the 328th in league play against other units and I was selected to play as a pitcher. I'm pretty excited about that. Our first practice was yesterday and I did okay.

I'm continuing to prepare for my teaching assignment. We don't have any books yet, but class starts in a few days, so I'm putting together my lesson plans without a book.

June 11 1945

Just got back from visiting Venice Rest Camp. Venice is unlike any place I've ever seen. All the historic buildings are intact. Other than one bombing run on the Germans' shipping docks, it is the only city the Germans occupied that the Allies never bombed or attacked.

The canals are something else. I had heard about them, but it is hard to imagine a place like that. Some of the boys rode the gondolas. The rest camp has some DUKWs that they use to take us on the canals for tour. We went to the beach area on Lido. It is a beautiful and unusual place. Hopefully I will get to come back.

12 June 1945

Classes started this afternoon and it went pretty good. Still no books, but almost all of the guys in the class grew up on farms (mostly in the South), so it wasn't hard to get started. These boys are all eager to get back to the farm.

Softball is good. I'm learning a lot playing with these guys. Don't know when we will start playing other units, but I think we will be ready.

This is so different here now without the fighting.   All are anxious to hear about going home.

13 June 1945

We've been relieved from our alert status, so looks like we won't be making the move east toward Yugoslavia.   Also, we've received word that the 85th will start preparing for shipment back to the U.S. in the near future and after arrival back in the U.S. the unit will be deactivated.   Good news for all of us!

Apparently too many officers and enlisted men are using postal money orders to send home large sums of money illegally obtained over here.   We were told today that no money orders will be written for an amount in excess of an individual's monthly pay and allowances, unless the commanding officer certifies that the money was obtained legally.   This probably should have been done a year ago.   The black market has been strong here for a while.   There are always people around working the angles to make money off of bad situations.

15 June 1945

A big group of us went on a scenic tour up to the Austrian border yesterday.   The Division has been putting these together for the last few days and yesterday was my turn.   The Italian Alps are really beautiful right now, but there is evidence of the war at various points along the route up there.   It is nice to go sightseeing in the mountains, instead of having to fight our way up and down them.   Makes it a lot easier to appreciate and admire the beauty of the area.   I especially enjoyed seeing the small farms in the Alpine valleys.   The meadows were green and watching the cattle grazing so peacefully was a pleasant sight for me. I have missed that that kind of peacefulness.

17 June 1945

Yesterday our first group of men left for home. 32 "high score" soldiers headed south to Naples to ship back to the U.S. The score is determined by how long you've been in the theater, how much combat, how many children you have, etc. The whole Division is still getting things ready to move south for shipment back home. No word on when everybody will go.

Last night the Division had an amateur talent contest. Some of these boys have real talent. It wouldn't surprise me if some of them don't become famous singers when we get back. It is pretty unbelievable to see these guys you've been fighting beside in the mud, get cleaned up and belt a song out like some of them did. It was a fun evening.

19 June 1945

We played our first league game today and won. I got to pitch a couple of innings in relief and did okay. It was a lot of fun.

Looks like the Army is starting to shake things up in preparation to shipping the division home. A couple of days ago, they transferred a group of high point personnel from the 10th Mountain Division to us here in the 85th. Then, today, 15 officers and 220 enlisted men with low scores were transferred to the 34th Infantry Division. All these moves, seem to point out the 85th is headed home soon!

CHAPTER SEVENTEEN
TO THE 34ᵀᴴ

20 June 1945

Looks like the Division is headed home, but not me. This evening, we received word that 4 officers and 105 enlisted men were being assigned from the 85ᵗʰ to the 34ᵗʰ Infantry Division – and I am one of the four officers. Capt. Dempsey said the Red Bulls needed some experienced, good men to bring them back up to strength, which I guess I should take as a compliment. But right now I don't. After all of this, all of the time with these boys, I get transferred out and they head home. I came over with them and I should be leaving with them. Leave it to the Army.

I'm assigned to Battery C, 125th Field Artillery Battalion of the 34ᵗʰ Infantry Division. Right now, they are in occupation of a coastal area west of here. I will be headed there tomorrow.

No one knows where the 34ᵗʰ will end up. Some units have already moved into Germany as an occupying force. We keep hearing of units heading to the Pacific. I'm ready to head home. Nothing I can do, but make the best of it though. I learned that much about being in the Army – you just have to make the best of whatever they send your way.

161

23 June 1945

I am in San Remo, Italy, in my new assignment with the 125ᵗʰ FA. The 34ᵗʰ Division is spread out over a pretty big area of occupation. We are in the "Italian Riviera" - a semi-tropical coastal area on the Mediterranean near France. If I can't go home, this is not a bad area to be stationed.

24 June 1945

We are quartered in a nice hotel that has been slightly shelled, but it's not in bad shape. The Battery Commander, Lt. Saucier, has instituted a program that all combat veterans in the battery should have full use of the hotel facilities. He set up with the manager of the hotel so that the men get to sit down at tables with linens on the table for supper each night. They can also get laundry & barber service within the hotel.

The men still go through the mess line with their mess kits, but they get to sit down on chairs in the hotel's dining room. It is a nice thing for the men who have been in combat so long. They appreciate it.

Softball is going strong here among the companies, so I'm going to try to play with the battalion team. I'm looking forward to that. Also, there are lots of passes for enlisted men and officers alike right now. There is a large rest camp at Allassio on the coast just east of here that is supposed to be one of the best. There is also a new Red Cross Club in Turin. Hopefully, I will have time to visit these soon.

30 June 1945

Seems every day brings more soldiers here from the 85th. The Army is mixing the Divisions all up trying to get some home and take care of what needs doing here in Europe and still fight the Japanese. I've been told the 85th is in the process of moving south toward Naples for shipment back home, but it isn't the same 85th Division that shipped over here. Over 300 officers and 6000 enlisted men have been transferred out of the 85th since the Germans surrendered and about 250 officers and 2500 enlisted men have transferred in from other Divisions to head home. So in effect the Custermen that I was a part of has been broken up.

The men of the 34th feel pretty much the same way. Lots of people coming and going in the Division as duties change from battle to occupation.

6 July 1945

This morning the battalion left San Remo and moved 114 miles north to Casalgrasso. We aren't far from Turin, near the Po River, in an area of northwest Italy I haven't been before.

163

12 July 1945

All of the officers were briefed today on what's next for the 34th Division.   We are to relieve the 10th Mountain Division and elements of the 91st Infantry Division in their role of controlling movement across the Morgan Line in Northeast Italy.   This is the same area near Trieste that the 85th was put on alert for a few weeks ago.   There has been a territorial dispute between Yugoslavia and U.S./Britain/Italy over who will control the area. The Morgan Line was established in June in an agreement between Yugoslavia and the U.S. and Britain.   While Yugoslavia was an ally against the Germans, the Russians are backing the Yugoslav's claim that that area should be part of their country. British and American leaders are supporting Italy's claim to the area.   The Morgan Line is a compromise that establishes a Yugoslav area and an Italian area.   There are both Italian & Slovenian people living in the area and apparently it has gone back & forth between countries over the years. We are to provide security in the zone and keep fighting from breaking out.

17 July 1945

The last couple of days, the entire division has been preparing for the move to Northeastern Italy, in the vicinity of Udine.

Today, we loaded battalion baggage onto a train at the Raccconigi railhead not far from here.   Most troops should leave tomorrow by train, but some of us will be driving in jeeps and trucks to our new location.

19 July 1945

The 125th FA troops traveling by train left Casalgrasso at 1600 hours on the 18th.   Our motor convoy left later that night and drove straight through.   We arrived near Grions, Italy, at about 1800 hours today.   It was a long drive across northern Italy. After it got light today, I recognized some of the area around Verona and toward Venice. I had been in this area with the 85th a

164

*couple of months ago. Made me think of my buddies in the 328th.
I hope they're all home now.*

*No problems on the drive except one of the jeeps from Battery A
wrecked last night. Apparently the driver fell asleep and ran off
the road and hit a tree. Put the jeep out of commission, but no
one was hurt. The rest of the battalion should be here by train
tomorrow.*

Tonight, I am in another place I've never heard of.

21 July 1945

*The train with the remainder of the troops arrived yesterday
morning. All men in the battery are settled in here. We are back
in a mountainous area and training for occupation and policing
duties.*

*All the boys are wondering what's next. With the war against the
Japanese continuing, some divisions have been redeployed to the
Pacific. The orientation film "On to Tokyo" was shown tonight in
the group movie area. Like "Two Down and One to Go," it was
too general to cast any light on the fate of individual soldiers, but
it did set forth army policy on redeployment & demobilization.
No one here wants to end up fighting in the Pacific.*

23 July 1945

*Yesterday we got word that some partisans have located an
ammo dump in our area. We moved to the dump and posted
guards. It was mainly German munitions that will be destroyed.*

*This whole border here has historically been an area of conflict.
It has been invaded by everybody from the Goths & Romans all
the way to the Nazis. And now we're here to keep the peace?
There is lots of tension among the various civilian groups in the
area – not to mention the Yugoslav troops.*

24 July 1945

We have specific rules that limit movement of anybody who is not registered as a citizen of this part of Italy. Any Yugoslav, Italian, or other nationality that wants to cross into our area without proper permits from the Allied Military Government (AMG) will be "politely but firmly refused admittance". Guess that sounds good to whoever wrote the rules, but it is a little different out here when you have to enforce it.

We have been training on enforcing the movement restrictions through identity checks, interrogations, and inspections of vehicles and baggage with "maximum tact and discretion". The Yugoslavs & Italians have a bad history here and just don't like each other. History & politics are making this all a touchy situation. Lots of guns and weapons everywhere.

This post-war occupation duty is sure different than a few months ago. More time for inspections & paperwork. Guess there is too much time on some folks hands so we have lots of administrative inspections. Things that didn't seem to matter so much in combat.

The good news is tomorrow I'm headed to the Trieste Rest Center for a few days.

29 July 1945

Another birthday in Italy and this one isn't too bad. I've been in Trieste for 3 days at the Army Rest Center.

Trieste is a nice city. It was controlled by Austria for years and they did a lot to develop the town and port. A lot of the buildings look like the pictures you see of Vienna. There is a big plaza on the waterfront where people gather. It is a nice place to visit.

The plaza faces the water to the west, so the sunsets over the water are nice. The staff at the rest center are very helpful. We've been able to see the sights and have enjoyed some good meals.

This is the biggest city in this zone and a big seaport – that is one of the reasons there has been conflict here over the years. Everybody wants control of the port.

Lt. Darnell (center) with a couple of buddies posing in front of "The Palace of Lloyd" on Trieste's waterfront piazza in 1945

31 July 1945

There was a big USO show last night at Cividale featuring the Andrews Sisters and Arther Treacher. Since I just got back from the Rest Center, I didn't go, but several from the 125th got to enjoy the show. They said that even though it rained, it was quite a performance.

Got a letter from Daddy last night. Wish it had been better news.

Doug stepped on a mine and lost his leg.   He had written me when I was in Camp Shelby and told me he had enlisted in the Marines. Doug has always been one of my favorite cousins. Poor Aunt Crecie – I know she is worried sick about him now. He is 5 years younger than me & now he is crippled for life. What's he going to be able to do with just one leg? That is going to be hard for him.   Maybe he is back at a hospital in the States by now. This war has messed up a lot of lives.

When I get home, can't wait to see everybody, but especially Mildred. I know there are lots of boys headed home now, and I hope none of them turn her head.   I know she is waiting for me, though. We have a special bond. There is no doubt in my mind that she is the one for me.

2 Aug 1945

This is really a different kind of duty here.   We've been helping the AMG capture civilians who are suspected of killing Italian political prisoners. Lots of old grudges and distrust among these people.   People are using this time to settle those grudges. Hundreds of people have disappeared in this area.   In addition to the ethnic differences, there are political groups like communists, socialists, fascists, etc. trying to gain control. It's a mess.

Weather has been mostly fair and warm here but last night it started raining and turned chilly. I've had enough Italian rain to last a lifetime.

7 Aug 1945

Stories are coming out about our use of a bomb of unbelievable power in Japan – an atomic bomb.   All the boys are hoping Japan will surrender now and this will end the war in the Pacific. That bomb sounds like a terrible thing. Surely Japan will surrender now.

8 Aug 1945

Looks like it is rainy season. Tonight there was a hail storm with hail over 1" in diameter. Luckily we are in buildings and not in tents. The hail was loud on the roof, but didn't do too much damage. It is good to be in a dry building and out of the weather.

10 Aug 1945

We heard that another atomic bomb was dropped yesterday on another town in Japan. I can't believe Japan hasn't surrendered yet. How many of their people will have to die for them to end this war? It's not just their soldiers now, but civilians too. We've been told the Russians have entered the war against Japan as well.

When will the world be tired of all of this killing? Those of us who have been in the middle of it have been tired of it a long time. So many people dead, so many lives ruined. I pray daily for Japan's surrender. With the stories we've heard from the Pacific, I can't imagine how bad it will be if our GIs have to go ashore & fight in Japan. I am worried for Carl and all the other boys there.

12 Aug 1945

Some of us got to go to a USO show at the Division CP tonight. Some big stars there like Allen Jones & Irene Harvey. It was an enjoyable show and a welcome break from our routine here. The USO and Red Cross have done a good job for us. All the soldiers appreciate them. I have to give the Army credit for providing entertainment for the boys who are still here on occupation duty.

14 Aug 1945

I'm in Venice tonight. Came down yesterday on the train. We will go back in a couple of days.

Venice is such an unusual place with the canals and water. I enjoy visiting here. This is my second time. The city is still like it has been for centuries.

After we got here yesterday we walked around Venice and we took one of the gondolas on the Grand Canal. One of the boys with us has never been here, so we did the boat ride for him. St. Mark's Square is a sight to see. You can sit there and drink coffee or wine and watch all the people go by. Lots of pretty girls. Lots of pigeons too!

Tonight we are at the Palazzo Al Mare on Lido Venice, which serves as an Allied Officers Rest Camp. It is a grand hotel right on the beach. I've never stayed anywhere like this. The Lido is a long narrow island, a big sandbar actually, that is across the lagoon from the city of Venice. We took a ferry over here and will go to the beach for a while tomorrow. The Lido is very different than Venice itself.

Seeing all the couples walking hand in hand here, really makes me miss Mildred more and more. One of these days, I will be able to take trips to places like this with her and we will walk hand in hand and laugh with each other.

In Lido Venice, Italy, August 15, 1945, in front of the Palazzo Al Mare

15 Aug 1945

What a great day today.

This morning we were at breakfast at the hotel when we heard the big news that Japan had finally surrendered! President Truman announced their surrender and all hostilities had ceased. The war is over! Finally. I thought about Carl and all the other boys in the Pacific. I said a silent prayer of thanks as everybody yelled and cheered. Men were slapping each other on the back, hugging, & smiling. Then over the loudspeaker came "God Bless America" and all of us stopped what we were doing and joined in. It gave me goose bumps.

We had a great time today at Lido. The beach was nice, with lots of people. Word had spread about Japan's surrender and everybody was in a great mood. We saw soldiers & sailors from several countries on Lido and shook hands with everyone. What a great day. Headed back up north on the train now.

18 Aug 1945

Even with Japan's surrender, our duty here continues. Nothing has changed in this dispute. In addition to our drills and regular training, we are getting more training on how to handle our occupation and policing duties. Everyone is relieved though that we won't be going to fight in the Pacific though. Now if we can just get back to the States soon.

We continue to train as artillerymen. There is a 105 range just north of here in Subit where we fire every few days.

25 Aug 1945

So WW2 began with disputes between countries over land that had changed ownership before and after WW1. One of these areas of dispute was right here where we are. So now WW2 is over and this land region is still in dispute. Tito's troops are pushing things to the brink of another war. They continue to threaten & harass us as we patrol our zone. We have strict instructions about what we can and can't do, but they seem to do what they want. This is different from combat, but it is still has us all on edge.

2 Sept 1945

The battalion had Catholic & Protestant church services this morning. It's been a peaceful, restful Sunday. Outside of our normal occupation and guard duties, tomorrow is a holiday for us in observance of both Labor Day and the formal signing of the Japanese surrender. None of us are use to holidays in the Army. No training or drills today or tomorrow. I'm going to use some of the time to catch up my letter writing. Tomorrow is Mildred's birthday, so I will send her a letter.

4 Sept 1945

Appointed to my first Court-Martial Board today. This is fairly routine duty for officers, with each serving his turn in defense counsel, trail judge advocate, and member of the court. I was appointed as trail judge advocate, which is the prosecutor. Looks like the next few days I will alternate between my other duties and court.

6 Sept 1945

Major Kimbrell, the 125th Commander, observed fire of our battery at the 105 range today. Everything went well.

We've received new training orders for the battery today as well. The new schedule cuts training to 6 hours per day for 5 ½ days a week. The main purpose of this new schedule is to attain proficiency in quelling civilian disturbances and to give the boys more opportunity to attend classes in preparation for post-war jobs. After two years of dreaming about what we will do when we get back home, it seems unreal that we are now actually making plans for our lives after the war.

I know what my plans are. When I get back, I'm going to ask Mildred to marry me. When the Army is done with me, I want to start a family with her. I want to farm our land and maybe have some cattle. I've always liked those Black Angus cattle. But the first thing is to get Mildred to say yes. After that, it will all fall into place.

10 Sept 1945

This Court-Martial Board duty makes me glad I'm not a lawyer. Luckily, most of the men plead guilty, so it goes pretty fast. Most of the cases seem to involve drinking too much, fighting, or theft. An occasional case involves an enlisted man disobeying an order or leaving his post. The Board should finish up tomorrow.

13 Sept 1945

Lt. Saucier told me tonight we will be making a move from Grions in a couple of days. The battalion is moving to the Gorizia area, about 25 miles south of here.

We continue to try to locate and guard ammo dumps. We have to keep the weapons out of the hands of the civilians. Different groups in this area just don't like each other. Part of our mission is to keep them from taking revenge and have a civil war start. Apparently this area has always been a powder keg waiting to explode.

14 Sept 1945

Good news for everybody today when we received word that the 34ᵗʰ Division will probably leave for the USA in late October or early November after culling out the low point men. As the news spread, you could see everybody's morale get a boost. We still have a job to do here, so we've got to keep the boys focused on their duty, even though you know they are thinking about going home.   I have to admit that that is what occupies my mind the most.

16 Sept 1945

Battery C moved to the Gorizia area today as an advance detail in preparation for the movement of the battalion.   The boys are set up and the next couple of days we will complete preparation for the others to arrive here.

19 Sept 1945

Lot happening today.   The remainder of the battalion displaced from Grions and arrived here at 1430 hours.   No incidents in the move and our advance preparations were in good shape.

I was assigned to Battery B as Battery Commander today as well. First battery commander post I've held, but I've had some good ones to learn from.   It will be pretty much more of the same type thing we've been doing in Battery C.   More occupation & security duties.

20 Sept 1945

We had a Battery Commander's meeting today to discuss regulations concerning our duties in the Gorizia area. We received instructions that we are going to be searching for and seizing illegal guns that are in possession of civilians in our zone. There is a lot of civil unrest here.   There have been riots in some towns, including Trieste.   The concern is that these weapons will cause problems for the Italian government when the area is handed back to them in the future.

We will be working with local police whenever possible and will be searching based on intelligence information only. Thank goodness we are not going house to house in the search.

22 Sept 1945

We've heard stories for months about the terrible things the Germans have done to Jews and other people in their prison camps. Today I saw a place near Trieste that was one of their prison & death camps. It was a terrible place. A big five story building that was an old rice-husking facility. The Nazis turned it into a prison, death chamber, and crematorium. We were told stories about what happened there. They shipped Jews and political prisoners into the place and then distributed them to the camps in Germany and Poland. Thousands came through there. It is estimated that about 5000 prisoners were executed at the place and cremated. When the Germans left the facility they tried to blow up the crematorium to destroy evidence of what they did, but they weren't successful. There is plenty of evidence of the killing of civilians here. Most were either shot or hit with a club at the base of the skull, then their bodies burned. Army investigators have been at this place for months piecing together the evidence. We've heard unbelievable stories from locals about what went on there.

I never want to go back to that place again.

1945 photo showing the former rice husking factory near Trieste that the Germans used as a detention center, prison, and crematorium. This photo shows where the Nazis attempted to destroy the crematorium as the war ended. Photo courtesy Civici Musei di Storia ed Arte

25 Sept 1945

The 88th Infantry Division will be replacing the 34th in this area. A couple of their artillery officers came here today to coordinate the relief of the 125th FA.   We are to begin handing over equipment & property to them and start our preparations for movement to the Naples Staging Area in the next few days.   It looks like we are headed home soon.

26 Sept 1945

I may not be going home soon after all. Nothing with the Army surprises me anymore. The battalion received Special Order #174 which stated that to be eligible to go home with the Division, officers must have a score of 85 or higher and enlisted men over 70. My score is 81. Because I am single with no children, my score isn't as high as some who haven't been over here as long.

Those of us who don't go home with the 34th will be transferred to the 88th Infantry Division. Am I ever going to get out of Italy??? My only hope is that this may not happen because the order does not become effective until October 1. I don't want to spend another winter here. The weather has turned cold. There was a big snowfall in the mountains last night. Today we were issued overcoats and winter underwear. They say winter in the Dolemites can be rough and it is looking like I will be here through it.

Soldiers of the 88th Infantry Division man a checkpoint along the Morgan Line with communist Yugoslavian soldiers on the other side. Photo from MtMestas.com.

28 Sept 1945

Some more elements of the 88th Division arrived yesterday in preparation for relieving the 34th. The division continues with preparations to move south to Naples as the first leg of the journey home. The men have been packing their personal equipment and we've been crating unit equipment that will go.

The last couple of days it's been hard to keep my disappointment at not going home with the Division from showing and affecting my duty. It was bad enough that I didn't get to go home with the 85th back in August and now I'm not going with the 34th either. But I've got a job to do in getting my boys ready to go. I just have to have faith it will all work out for me. I've made it this far and I'm alive, so I know it is just a matter of time before I'm back home.

29 Sept 1945

My prayers have been answered! I'm going home with the Division after all. We got a last minute announcement today that the critical score for officers to go home with the Division has been lowered to 75. I will be on the ship with the Red Bulls heading back to the USA. Those of us this affected didn't have much time to pack, but who needed it? I've been ready for months.

Trucks showed up this evening and our duffle backs were loaded in preparation for the move tomorrow morning. My journey home starts in the morning.

CHAPTER EIGHTEEN
THE JOURNEY HOME

30 Sept 1945

It's Sunday and I am in a truck convoy headed to the USA via the Naples Staging Area. I like writing that – headed to the USA! Been waiting a long time to write that in this notebook.

We got up early and assembled for breakfast at 0330 hours this morning. Then everybody loaded onto trucks and the convoy headed south. Lots of chatter among the boys – almost like a bunch of school kids. We are starting our journey home. The feeling is hard to describe. 800 miles to Naples.

1 Oct 1945

We arrived in Naples late yesterday evening. Driving south, we passed through a lot of the country that we had fought through when we were chasing the Nazis northward. My thoughts were filled with memories of the things that happened along the way. Some good thoughts, but a lot of thoughts I wish I could forget. If I ever have children, I hope they never have to go to war.

The 125ᵗʰ FA is housed at the University of Naples, which isn't bad. Everybody is squared away here and now it is just a matter of time before we ship home.

We will continue to drill and train and attempt to get back to more of a spit & polish unit as we prepare to go back to the States.

181

4 Oct 1945

Naples looks a lot better than when I came through here 18 months ago. While the effect of the war is obvious, the water & electricity are working and people have re-opened shops. There is still lots of debris, but it is getting cleaned up. It smells better. People are rebuilding.

We get passes to visit Naples and the surrounding area, but most men aren't that interested in sightseeing in Italy anymore. The only sight most want to see is the USA.

The liberal passes give the boys something to do, but also give a chance for a few to find trouble. I've got a handful in my battery I know to keep an eye on. I plan on keeping my men out of any trouble and getting them all on that boat home.

6 Oct 1945

We continue to do some training to maintain discipline, but a couple of hours each day are spent in various classes to prepare the enlisted men for civilian life in the states. There are plenty of passes available to visit the city and local area.

Yesterday a few of us went to a little inlet on the north end of Naples Bay to swim and spend the day. Not many people were there and we had a good time. One of the Florida boys with us found some oysters. He showed us how to open & eat them raw. We waded out into a shallow part of the bay and had a small feast. Popping them open with our knives and eating them fresh right there! I've never done that before. They were good – salty and fresh tasting like the sea.

9 Oct 1945

Apparently, the Army is concerned with discipline as we get ready to head home. Complaints about KP, guard, and cleaning duty are pretty common now. A directive came to us reminding everybody that even though we are headed home we are still on full duty status and that we will be called upon to work. Waiting around and cleaning up are not the favorite things for a soldier, but both are a big part of life in the Army. The men are restless, eager to go home.

15 Oct 1945

Everybody has been sweating out sailing time the last week or so. Rumors are flying around about when we will set sail. You can hear about anything, but it's best not to believe anything until you get the order.

It is a big job getting thousands of men ready to go home and everything in order. Special units have been set up that check division supply and personnel records to make sure everything and everybody is in line. If the paperwork isn't right, then you don't get on the boat. We have to make sure that we have all the paperwork for our men squared away, so I've been spending more time working on that.

20 Oct 1945

Two days ago ended all the passes as we are getting processed to ship home. Today all the baggage belonging to enlisted men and officers was inspected for customs clearance. Sailing date is set for October 22.

Yesterday I had to go through the men in my battery and check for any extra guns & souvenirs they had picked up during the fighting. We are allowed to take one personal souvenir gun home, so I had to go inspect each man's duffel in the battery.

I gave them the opportunity to try to sell any extra guns they had before I went back through their things again this morning to make sure they were okay. I had to sell a little .25 caliber Italian gangster pistol myself. I picked it up when we were in Trieste. It was nice – had pearl handles and would fit in the palm of your hand. I was going to give it to Daddy, but I would rather take the luger I got off of the SS Colonel home. I found an Air Corp pilot who wanted it and sold it for $100.00. Those Air Corp guys have been buying several of the boys' extra guns. Guess they have plenty of money and no souvenirs.

22 Oct 1945

The USS Monticello steamed out of Naples harbor this morning and I'm onboard. It is hard to believe we are finally headed home.

Even with the joy of leaving, it is hard not to think of our buddies we lost that will never leave Italy. Good men whose families will never see them again. Watching the shore move away, flooded with memories of the things that happened here, I said a prayer for those boys and their families. I also bowed my head and thanked God for bringing me through this. Lots of emotions as we pulled out of Naples harbor.

There was a lot different attitude among everybody walking up the gangplank here than when we left the U.S. a couple of years ago. We've all aged and grown up a lot. War has changed all of us. It seems like such a long time since I arrived in Italy.

The Monticello is about the same size as the Anderson that we left the U.S. in – maybe a little bigger. It has a Coast Guard crew instead of Navy. Seeing the Coast Guard sailors, I thought about Geraldine and her Coast Guard boyfriend. Guess I will get to meet him sometime soon. I wonder if Daddy knows about him yet.

I heard the Monticello was originally an Italian ocean liner that was converted for troop transport. I can believe it because it has a different layout from the ship we came over on. It's still crowded, but better than the trip over. Little things don't seem to matter so much right now.

USS Monticello in 1945

24 Oct 1945

It has taken a couple of days to reach Gibraltar It is quite an impressive sight as we passed through the Straits The Mediterranean has been beautiful - smooth and calm as we left Italy. As we entered the Atlantic though it was a different story. You could actually see a big difference of how rough the Atlantic looked compared to the Mediterranean. And sure enough it is a lot rougher.

The food is good on this trip. Last night we had steak! And cold milk! We haven't had milk since we left the U.S. It tasted so good that I drank three glasses.

27 Oct 1945

We get to spend more time on deck on the Monticello than we did when we shipped overseas. We still have lifeboat drills, but there is no danger from enemy aircraft and submarines, so there is a big difference in the restrictions. There is a chill in the air out here, but it is better on the deck than down below.

1 Nov 1945

We got word today that the 34th Division will be de-activated once we arrive in the U.S. Most of the enlisted men will be mustered out. Officers will be handled differently. My orders say that I will need to report to Fort McPherson near Atlanta where I will get my next duty assignment. After we arrive at Ft. Patrick Henry and get the enlisted men taken care of, I should get leave and can go home to Alabama before I have to report to Ft. McPherson. I can't wait to get on that train headed south!

2 Nov 1945

We should be docking at Hampton Roads early tomorrow.

All day long today the men hugged the rail on the ship...everybody just wanting to stand there and watch the water...thinking how good it is going to be...thinking who to call and going home. Thinking of how it is going to be to crawl into fresh, clean sheets at home for the first time...thinking how peaceful the world seems now.

Even though its late at night now, boys are still lining the rails...no one wants to go to bed... our thoughts are so much on home...on the folks...on wives' & girlfriends, on everything that goes with home... on home-cooked meals and chocolate malts. Everybody is talking about the first thing they are going to do when they get home.

As always, Mildred is on my mind. She seems to be more and more as we get closer to home. I can't wait to see her. In a few days, I will be able to put my arms around her. When I get off the boat, I'm going to call her, then Daddy, and Geraldine. It will be good to hear their voices.

My mind keeps running back on all the things that happened "over there". The unbelievable tough times, some of the terrible things, but there were some fun times with buddies too. I became friends with some good men. Men I will always respect and share a bond with. But how can I ever forget about the ones that will never be coming back. Even with the excitement of coming home, you can't forget about them. I guess they will be in my mind forever.

Time to try to get some sleep, but I believe it's going to be hard to do. Big day tomorrow. Everybody is as excited as kids on Christmas Eve!

3 Nov 1945

A big group of us were up on deck as the sun came up and showed us the shoreline of the east coast. What a sight! It is hard to describe the feeling as we entered the harbor at Hampton Roads. There was a Navy band playing as we docked. I believe every member of the 34ᵗʰ Division was on the rail, smiling & cheering. Don't think I will ever forget those moments. Back in the U.S.A.!

The efficiency of the transportation corps in unloading this huge shipment of men was pretty amazing. It was done without a hitch. In no time the men were comfortably set in barracks at Ft. Patrick Henry. Earlier tonight we were treated to the best meal I've have had while in the army.

We were able to make some telephone calls tonight. I called Mildred, and then Daddy & Geraldine. It was good to hear their voices. I can't believe I will see them soon! The conversation with Mildred didn't last long enough. Just hearing her voice made me feel like a new man. I'm smiling just thinking about her now. Can't wait to see her.

So this is the first night I will spend on American soil in almost two years. I am so grateful to God that He watched over me while I was overseas. I'm alive and headed home to Alabama soon.

This is my last journal entry. Writing down things that were happening and my thoughts helped me through my time overseas, but I am back in America now. Time to leave the war behind and start my new life. Based on what we've been told, we should all be home in a few days.

CHAPTER NINETEEN
SHE'S WITH ME

November 9, 1945

"I didn't go halfway around the world, fight a war and come home to lose the only girl I ever loved," thought B.B. as he set his jaw and turned across the railroad tracks onto Beehive Road.

A few minutes later, B.B. turned off Wire Road onto the sandy lane that led down to the Moore's house. He saw Mr. Moore out in the yard. Mildred's daddy was a raw-boned, tough sawmill man who had raised seven tough boys and one very pretty girl. And that girl was extra special to her daddy.

B.B. took a deep breath as he pulled the truck to a stop. He wasn't sure what Mr. Moore would think of him showing up like this.

"Hey boy, good to see you back safe and sound," Mr. Moore said as he shook B.B.'s hand.

"Yes sir, it's good to be home. Is Mildred here? I need to see her." B.B. didn't want to beat around the bush, he had to do what he had to do.

"Well, B.B., she is in the house getting ready to go out. I don't think she can see you now."

189

B.B. gathered himself up to his full height, mustered everything he had in him, looked Mr. Moore in the eye and said "No Sir, I need to see her right now. She is going out with me tonight."

Mr. Moore held B.B.'s gaze for a couple of seconds and said "Well she didn't tell me anything about that."

"She doesn't know yet," B.B. said quickly.

Mr. Moore's eyes crinkled with the slightest hint of a smile as he said "Wait on the porch" and turned to go in the house.

B.B.'s heart was pounding as fast as it ever had in the heat of battle as he stood on that porch for what seemed like an eternity. Standing there, he was using all the tricks he had learned in the war to remain calm, breath, and maintain control. Just then, the screen door opened and Mildred came out smiling, looking better than anything B.B. had seen in his entire life. Seeing Mildred's smile and her face light up at the moment their eyes met was everything he had dreamed about while overseas. As they hugged, a warmth came over B.B. that would last a lifetime. He couldn't stop smiling as he finally, finally got to see his "Dearest Mildred". At that moment, he knew without a doubt that this was the woman for him.

Mr. and Mrs. Moore (both smiling as well) came out of the house to keep a watchful eye on them as B.B. pulled Mildred aside. B.B.'s heart was racing as fast as his words as he told Mildred about his feelings for her. He told her that he wanted to be with her forever, starting with a date right now! Mildred blushed, smiled, and replied that she wanted to go out with him too. B.B.'s smile turned into a full blown grin, "then let's get going," he told her.

B.B. was walking on air as they headed towards the porch steps. Mildred paused and told her parents that she was going to go with B.B. and would be back later that evening. She wasn't sure what they were thinking about her decision, but at that moment, she didn't care.

As B.B. held the truck door open for Mildred and helped her in, Mr. Moore said, "Well George will be here soon to pick you up. What am I supposed to say?"

"Tell'em she's with me," B.B. replied to Mildred's father as he got in the truck with her and began his new life.

EPILOGUE

B.B.'s simple, confident reply was the truth of a lifetime. *"Tell'em she's with me."* And she was, from that moment on.

B.B. & Mildred got married two weeks later and were by each other's side for over 65 years until his death on May 28, 2011.

Mildred & B.B. Darnell on their wedding day, November 21, 1945

APPENDIX A

Map of Lt. B.B. Darnell's Journey in Italy

Lt. B. B. Darnell's Journey Through Italy

1   March 27, 1944 Arrive in Naples
2   April 12, 1944 Entered battle for the first time near Minturno
3   May 15-16 1944 Actions earned Silver Star near
    Castellonorato
4   June 5 1944 Entered Rome
5   July 28 1944 Near Volterra
6   August 18, 1944 Near San Miniato overlooking Arno River
7   September 10 1944 Moved through Florence
8   September 11 1944 Saw Gothic Line for first time
9   September 15- October 3 1944   Actions earned Oak Leaf
    Cluster to Silver Star in area
10 October 12, 1944 Wounded in action near Monterenzio
11 December 23 1944 Moved to north of Lucca in anticipation of
    German offensive in Western Coastal Section
12 January 10 1945 moved back into mountains north of
    Florence
13 April 15, 1945 in position in mountains near Abba as Spring
    Offensive against Gothic Line begins
14 April 21 1945   entered Po Valley
15 April 29 1945 on outskirts of Verona
16 May 2 1945 in Italian Alps near Gron as German army in Italy
    surrenders
17 May 30 1945 85th Division moves to assembly area near Pez
18 June 23 1945 Transferred from 85th Division to 34th Division
    and arrived in San Remo
19 July 17 1945 34th Division moved to northeast Italy in the area
    of Trieste
20 September 30 1945   Leaves Trieste as 34th Division begins trip
    home
21 October 1 1945   Arrives in Naples
22 October 22 1945   Left Naples headed for USA

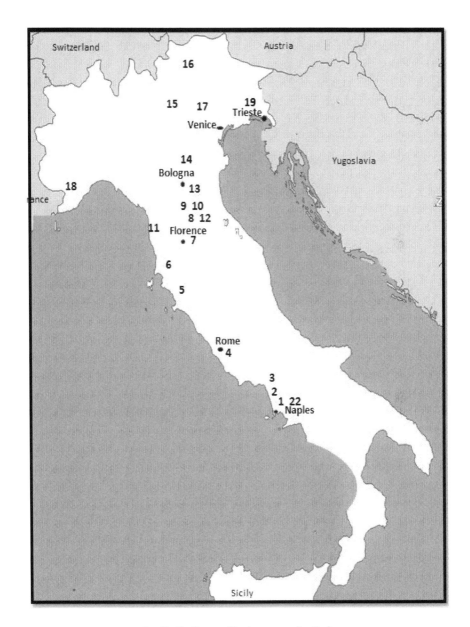

Lt. B. B. Darnell's Journey in Italy

APPENDIX B

Glossary of Terms and Abbreviations

105s - The 105 Howitzer was one of the newest American artillery guns at the onset of WWII. Seven men were needed to operate a 105. The gun had a range of just over 7 miles

API – Alabama Polytechnic Institute located in Auburn, AL. The name was later changed to Auburn University.

Battalion - A military unit smaller than a division. In World War II an artillery battalion (like the 328th Field Artillery) consisted of approximately 500 men with three firing batteries and support units

Battery - A battery is an actual firing unit of the artillery battalion. In WWII a 105 mm howitzer battery would consist of approximately 100 men and usually had four 105 mm howitzer artillery guns.

Bivouac - traditionally refers to a military encampment made with tents or improvised shelters.

CO - Commanding Officer of a unit

C Rations - The C-Ration was an individual canned, pre-cooked, and prepared wet ration. It was intended to be issued for U.S. military land forces when fresh food (A-ration) or packaged unprepared food (B-ration) prepared in mess halls or field kitchens was impractical or not available.

Casualty -- This term applies to any person who is lost to a military unit by having died of wounds or disease, having received wounds, or having been injured but not mortally.

Corps - Divisions were normally grouped into corps, for commitment to combat. A corps consisted of at least two divisions, but usually contained several, at least one of which was an armored division. Divisions were "attached" rather than "assigned" to a corps and were frequently moved from corps to corps as the combat situation dictated.

Division - The infantry division was the smallest Army organization deemed capable of conducting independent combat operations, as virtually all ground combat and support capabilities were possessed by units assigned to the division.   During WWII an infantry division consisted of approximately 15,000 men, including infantry and artillery battalions as well as medical, signal, and engineer units.

DUKW - A six-wheel drive amphibious truck used by the Army in World War II for transportation of goods and troops over land and water.

FA - Field Artillery

Fascist - In Italy, a follower of Benito Mussolini. Fascists sought to unify their nation through an authoritarian state. Fascist ideology consistently invokes the primacy of the state over the individual citizen

Gustav Line - The Gustav Line was a line of German military fortifications in southern Italy during World War II. It ran across Italy from north of where the Garigliano River flows into the Tyrrhenian Sea in the west, to the mouth of the Sangro River on the Adriatic coast in the east. The Gustav Line was fortified with concrete bunkers, gun pits, machine-gun pillboxes, minefields, anti-tank obstacles, and barbed wire, and was held by 15 divisions of the German Army.

Gothic Line - The Gothic Line formed the German Army's last major line of defense in the final stages of World War II along the summits of the northern part of the Apennine Mountains during the fighting retreat of the German forces in Italy against the Allied Armies in Italy. Using more than 15,000 slave-laborers, the Germans created more than 2,000 well-fortified machine gun nests, casemates, bunkers, observation posts and artillery-fighting positions to repel any attempt to breach the Gothic Line.

LCVP - Landing Craft Vehicle Personnel or Higgins boat was a landing craft used extensively in amphibious landings in World War II.

K Rations - The K-ration was an individual daily combat food ration which was introduced by the United States Army during World War II. It was originally intended as an individually packaged daily ration for mobile forces for short durations. The K-ration provided three separately boxed meal units: breakfast, dinner (lunch) and supper (dinner).

Mess – refers to the soldiers' meals or food in the military. A mess kit is the soldier's plate, cup, utensils, etc.   A mess hall is where the meals are served.

OP - Observation Post

Registration – As it applies to field artillery, it is the process of calibrating & setting up the guns by firing at an accurately know point.

V-Mail - At the beginning of WWII, overseas delivery of mail was slow and erratic. Then the military began encouraging Americans to use V-mail. Letters were addressed and written on a special one-sided form, sent to Washington where they were opened and read by army censors, then photographed onto a reel of 16 mm microfilm.

The reels – each containing some 18,000 letters – were then flown overseas to receiving stations. There, each letter was printed onto a sheet of 4-inch by 5-inch photographic paper, slipped into an envelope and bagged for delivery to the front.

XO - Battery Executive Officer.   The Battery Executive Officer was usually a lieutenant, with the Battery Commanding Officer being a Captain. In many cases, the executive officer ran day-to-day operations and oversaw all firing sequences and missions

APPENDIX C

Units to Which Lt. Darnell was Assigned While Overseas

85th Infantry Division (Custer Division) - The 85th Infantry Division
was the second all-draftee infantry division to see combat in World War
II. The division was named after George Armstrong Custer, a native of
Michigan where the division was activated in 1917 for service during
World War I. The 85th was re-activated at Camp Shelby, Mississippi in
May 1942

The Division would have included approximately 15,000 men.

The 85th Division was comprised of three infantry regiments (337th,
338th, & 339th), four field artillery battalions (328th, 329th, 403rd, &
910th), plus other support units such as medical, engineer, and signal.

B.B. Darnell was a member of the 85th Division, 328th Field Artillery until
June 20, 1945.

328th Field Artillery Battalion - The 328th Field Artillery Battalion was a
part of the 85th Infantry Division.

Each battalion had three firing batteries (usually 4 guns each), a
Headquarters Battery (the CO and his staff along with fire direction
personnel, communications center, etc.) and a Service Battery
(ammunition, basic supplies, mechanics, etc).

A 105 mm battalion contained just over 500 men. Each battery in the
battalion had about 100 men, usually 5 officers and 95 enlisted men.

Battalions were usually headed by a lieutenant colonel with an executive officer who was usually a major. Batteries were usually headed by a captain with a executive officer who was a lieutenant.

B.B. Darnell was attached to Battery C (Charlie Battery) of the 328th Field Artillery.

34th Infantry Division (Red Bulls) - The 34th Division was one of the first US divisions to be sent to Europe and saw more combat service than almost any US division: 500 days. After the German surrender, its mission consisted of occupying the Northeast Italy area along what was known as the Morgan Line near Trieste in a "stand-off" with Russian-backed Yugoslavian forces wanting to annex the area. This was one of the first confrontations of the coming "Cold War"

B.B. Darnell served in the 34th Infantry Division from June 20, 1945 until his return to the U.S. in November, 1945

125th Field Artillery Battalion

The 125th FA was a part of the 34th Infantry Division. After he was reassigned from the 85th Division in mid-June, 1945, B.B. Darnell served as a Battery Executive Officer with Battery C until mid-September when he became Commanding Officer for Battery B.

Author's Note of Thanks

My gratitude extends to so many people who helped me along the way as I worked on this book, including:

My family *who encouraged and supported the endeavor. The enthusiasm and interest of my children as I shared information I discovered about their grandfather, kept me digging for more.*

Sons & daughters of members of the 328th Field Artillery *whose words, photographs, and direction were essential to this happening, specifically:*

> **Steve Cole***, who has done massive amounts of research on the 85th Infantry Division. Steve gave me access to everything in his website and was always willing to answer my questions. His hero father, Staff Sgt. Newton F. Cole was in Battery B of the 328th FA. I have no knowledge of his father's interaction with my father, but I know they were at a 1986 reunion together, as was Steve. Steve was a great resource in this work.*

> **Bill Dempsey***, whose hero father, Capt. William Dempsey, was not only the CO of Battery C, but he was also a friend of my father's during their time in the 328th. Bill provided me with great photographs from our fathers' time overseas as well as some stories shared by his father.*

> **Patricia Corbett***, whose hero father was Sgt. Walter Keane of Battery A of the 328th FA. Sgt. Keane faithfully wrote home to his wife and his wife saved every letter. Pat has those letters and generously shared some of the information from them with me.*

*The only surviving hero of the 328th FA that I was able to speak with was **Harold Goodwin** who was the CO of the Service Battery in the 328th FA.   Mr. Goodwin lives on Long Island, NY, and I was honored to be able to speak with him by telephone.   While he did not remember my father, he was very gracious as he answered my questions about his wartime experiences.*

*The generous and kind Italian people I met while re-tracing my father's steps in Italy.   Special thanks and gratitude to the **Poletti family** at Futa Pass.   Their hospitality, kindness, and encouragement made a dreary day in the Apennine Mountains become a point of inspiration in my quest.*

*Numerous government officials, from **Congressman Brett Guthrie** and his staff member **Gregg Reynolds** in Bowling Green, KY, all the way to employees at the National Archives and various Army facilities who assisted me in locating information.*

***Mrs. Kitty Sanders**, a retired English teacher, who contributed her time and expertise to my efforts by proof-reading my manuscript.*

*My friend, **Susan Baxter**, who encouraged me every step of the way.   As my travel partner in Italy, she was happy to forego the more traditional tourist sites so that we could explore the small towns and rural areas where my father had spent most of his time during the war.   Her advice and perspective was invaluable.   Her emotional involvement in the project is evidenced by her poem "I Can Remember" which she penned after reading the first draft of my father's story.*

Thanks to all of you and the many others who gave me an encouraging word or bit of information in my journey to document my father's wartime experience.

With eternal appreciation for those who served…

Alone, at this WWII British Commonwealth Cemetery near Minturno, Italy, in August, 2014, I knelt in a silent prayer of gratitude that my father made it back home to Alabama. I thanked God for the sacrifices of all who fought, and I prayed He would bless the families of those who never made it home.

Mike Darnell
April 10, 2015

42134194R00129

Made in the USA
Charleston, SC
16 May 2015